The
FRIENDSHIP
BOOK
of Francis Gay

A THOUGHT
FOR EACH DAY
IN 2005

D. C. THOMSON & CO., LTD.
London Glasgow Manchester Dundee

*Friendship is the golden thread
that ties the heart of all the world.*

John Evelyn.

January

SATURDAY — JANUARY 1.

"I DO hope," said Margo, pinning a new calendar on the wall of her kitchen, "that this year turns out better than the last. Do you remember that awful Spring cold I had, the Summer holiday when my luggage got lost and it rained every day, and then in November the central heating broke down one bitterly cold evening . . ?"

"Ah, but don't forget," interrupted husband Jonathan, "it was also the same year in which we had a magnificent display of daffodils, a Summer full of picnics and outings, and then in the Autumn, a really enjoyable and unexpected weekend in Paris."

For a moment Margo looked abashed, then she grinned. "I do hope," she began again as she made the calendar secure, "that this year turns out just as well as the last one did!"

It's always worth remembering that life can be as good or as bad as the way in which we choose to perceive it!

SUNDAY — JANUARY 2.

FOR the Lord giveth wisdom: out of his mouth cometh knowledge and understanding.

Proverbs 2:6

MONDAY — JANUARY 3.

ANOTHER year brings to our notice the annual January custom of new resolutions made for the next twelve months. Our neighbour John showed us his list and says he has — for the moment! — every intention of keeping most of these intact:

I will give up complaining and be more grateful.
I will give up pessimism and be an optimist.
I will stop judging harshly and think kind
*   thoughts.*
I will give up worry and trust in providence.
I will give up discouragement and be full of hope.
I will give up bitterness and turn to forgiveness.
I will give up anger and practise being patient.
I will give up gossiping and control my tongue.
I will give up being gloomy and enjoy the beauty
*   that is around me.*

TUESDAY — JANUARY 4.

OF all the many blessings of this world, I would rate the gift of friendship as being one of the greatest. I came across these quotes, penned by writers whose birthplaces are separated by the Atlantic yet both sum up perfectly the essence of true friendship:

"So long as we are loved by others I should say that we are almost indispensable; and no man is useless while he has a friend."

Robert Louis Stevenson.

"A friend is a person with whom I may be sincere. Before him I may think aloud."

Ralph Waldo Emerson.

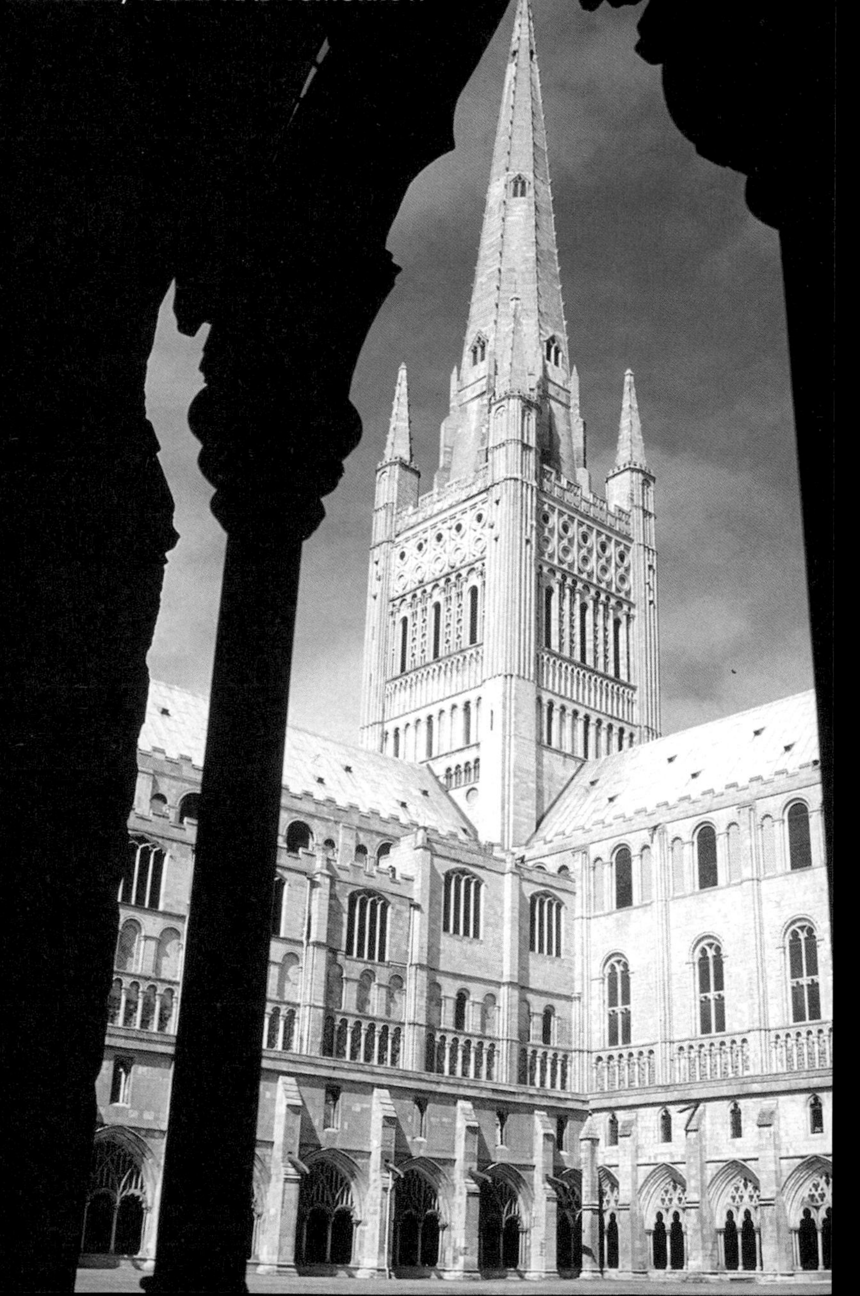

WEDNESDAY — JANUARY 5.

MY thought for today in these early days of a New Year comes from the pen of that well-loved Scottish poet Robert Burns, who is revered the world over. These lines are full of experience and love of life:

Then catch the moments as they fly
And use them as ye ought, man!
Believe me, Happiness is shy,
And comes not ay when sought, man!

THURSDAY — JANUARY 6.

MR JONES is a retired clergyman whom I've known for some time and, as his name suggests, he is Welsh. He spent a few days in his native Cardiff which he hadn't visited for some years and later I asked, "Did you enjoy your trip?"

"A challenge," he replied, "so many changes — new buildings, new one-way systems — it took me ages to find my way about. I felt lost." He thought for a moment, then added:

"You know, I could make a sermon out of that comment! Those observations apply to life as a whole. There are constant changes; we may feel ill at ease with them, and family life always holds many challenges.

"Well, isn't it good to realise that God does not change — He encourages us to face up to the changes we experience . . . His love is the same as it has always been and will remain constant."

Mr Jones then recalled the apt line from Henry Francis Lyte's well-loved hymn "Abide With Me": "Oh, thou who changest not . . ."

FRIDAY — JANUARY 7.

OUR friend Sheila, who teaches in Sunday school, asked one of her pupils: "Now tell me truthfully, Craig — do you say your prayers before eating?"

"No," he replied. "I don't have to. My mother is a good cook!"

Doesn't this prove that, no matter how serious or light-hearted the question, an honest answer is always the best one to give?

SATURDAY — JANUARY 8.

OH, have you got a minute?
Just a moment of your day,
For here's a chance to spend it
In a very useful way:
You could call an old acquaintance
And catch up on their news,
You could natter to a neighbour,
And dissolve away their blues.
You could make a child feel special
Just by taking time to hear
All the things they burst to tell you,
Every hope and every fear.
You could smile upon a stranger
Who is feeling at a loss,
You could build a bridge of kindness
And invite them then to cross.
For you see, in just a minute,
Though it may be all you've got,
If you use that minute wisely,
You'll achieve an awful lot.

Margaret Lyall.

SUNDAY — JANUARY 9.

AND, behold, the whole city came out to meet Jesus.

Matthew 8:34

MONDAY — JANUARY 10.

AS I was clearing snow from our path after a heavy snowfall, a neighbour called a greeting with the words, "This lot will be slush by the morning!"

It doesn't take long, does it, for our appreciation of a simple snowfall to turn to irritation at the mess and chaos that follows? Yet, if we stopped to consider the delicate and individual beauty of each snowflake, perhaps we wouldn't be so quick to complain.

As a child growing up in the snowbelt of the United States' Vermont, Wilson "Snowflake" Bentley loved snow more than anything. When he was fifteen years old, he was given a microscope, and was stunned by what he saw when he examined the snow under it.

He learned to photograph individual snowflakes and, by the time he died in 1931, was the world's expert on them. His beautiful images are surely an enduring reminder of God's crystal miracles.

TUESDAY — JANUARY 11.

A TIME-WORN proverb from Arabia advises: "Write the bad things that are done to you in sand, but write the good things that happen to you on a piece of marble."

Good advice!

FROSTED FILIGREE

WEDNESDAY — JANUARY 12.

IT'S always a pleasure to bump into our old friend Mary because she has a smile for everyone. I once complimented her on this and she laughed.

"When I was young," she said, "my mother impressed upon me that when I went out each day, not only should I look clean and tidy, I should also make sure I was wearing a pleasant expression — for others would notice if I forgot. It probably sounds old-fashioned advice nowadays, but I think it's stood me in good stead."

I think so, too. Let's all try to emulate that particular habit.

THURSDAY — JANUARY 13.

AS a young child Amy once spent most of her holiday pocket money on a brooch for a favourite aunt. She thanked her for it, but Amy never saw Aunt Flo wear it, and at a later date Amy saw it, still in its packaging, in a jewellery box. She felt hurt.

Years later, Aunt Flo died, and it fell to the family to sort out her effects. Once more Amy discovered the brooch, still in the same box.

But by then her perspective had changed. No doubt the brooch had not been to Aunt Flo's taste, but what mattered was the fact that it had been kept carefully all those years, stored with her other treasures.

The facts don't change over the years, but the way we interpret them often does.

FRIDAY — JANUARY 14.

JOAN and Carol had been friends for a long time until a small disagreement somehow led to a distancing between them. Then Joan tripped and broke her wrist — an unlucky event, but one which gave Carol the chance to drop by, bearing flowers and offers of practical help.

Now Joan's wrist is fully healed, and so is her relationship with Carol. "I was told," said Joan, "that when a bone breaks, the healing process often makes it end up even stronger than it was before. I'm sure friendships can be like that as well."

I agree, but let us all try to make it a rule not to wait for broken bones before we start mending bridges!

SATURDAY — JANUARY 15.

HERE is a Chinese proverb I hadn't heard before. It successfully conveys a number of wise thoughts that deserve to be shared:

If there is light in the soul, there will be beauty in the person.
If there is beauty in the person, there will be harmony in the house.
If there is harmony in the house, there will be order in the nation.
If there is order in the nation, there will be peace in the world.

SUNDAY — JANUARY 16.

IF any man have ears to hear, let him hear.
Mark 7:16

THE FRIENDSHIP BOOK

MONDAY — JANUARY 17.

FOR years Bill eagerly looked forward to retirement. "I'm not going to do a thing," he used to say. "I'll do absolutely nothing!"

Well, Bill is now retired and when I met him one afternoon he was in a great hurry.

"Oh, I soon got tired of doing nothing," he explained. "I'm as busy as I ever was. It's wonderful!"

And he dashed off to a charity meeting, a busy — and happy — man.

TUESDAY — JANUARY 18.

A FRIEND in Sweden sent me this verse from his church magazine:

Out in the park he munched his roll and said,
"What difference do I make, alive or dead?
I count for less with every day that comes."
But he did not see the birds that ate his crumbs.

We all make a difference, even when we don't realise it.

WEDNESDAY — JANUARY 19.

WE don't talk so much about duty nowadays. The word has a cold ring and people tend to avoid it. But should we?

General Robert E. Lee described duty as "the sublimest word in the language". George Herbert said that duty performed "gives us music at midnight". And Robert Louis Stevenson declared: "There is no duty we so much underrate as the duty of being happy."

So bring back duty!

THE FRIENDSHIP BOOK

THURSDAY — JANUARY 20.

LOOKING before us —
We see only the road ahead.
Looking behind us —
We see only the shadows of the past.
But looking around us —
We see beauty, friendship, love and laughter.
Enjoy the present —
And the wonderful world around us!

Iris Hesselden.

FRIDAY — JANUARY 21.

I ONCE spoke to a friend who had been travelling in South America. Amid the extraordinary splendour of mountain landscape she found the direst poverty. It was particularly traumatic for her to witness the suffering of young children.

One day a little girl came running up to her. She didn't beg for money or ask for food — she simply held her hand tightly.

It's easy to forget that what people need most in the world cannot be satisfied by material things alone. What they ask of us is love.

SATURDAY — JANUARY 22.

THERE have been, over the years, many ideas about how to overcome the ever-present problem of worrying about this and that. This advice was handed down through the generations in a friend's family:

"Worry is the 'darkroom' in which 'negatives' are developed."

SUNDAY — JANUARY 23.

AND it shall be our righteousness, if we observe to do all these commandments before the Lord our God, as he hath commanded us.

Deuteronomy 6:25

MONDAY — JANUARY 24.

IT was a cold, grey and wet Winter's day. More like November than January, and daylight hours were still very short. New Year was behind us with all its hope and promise, and Spring seemed far away.

As the Lady of the House and I walked home in the gloom one afternoon, we suddenly saw a splash of colour in a small garden. Quite taken aback, we stopped and looked closely. There was a colourful patch of pansies — yellow, purple and white. They stood out against the black earth and sodden grass.

Of course, they, too, were a little wet and had been buffeted by the recent wind, but their faces still seemed bright and smiling. Considerably cheered by the sight, we went on our way, giving thanks, as always, to Mother Nature.

Perhaps Spring wasn't quite so far away after all!

TUESDAY — JANUARY 25.

NO-ONE quite knows how eels reach the Sargasso Sea. But we know they do all the same — no scientist would deny it.

That's what faith is, believing in what you know to be true, even though that belief can't always be proved by the tests of science.

WEDNESDAY — JANUARY 26.

THE twentieth-century writer John Creasey received a grand total of 774 rejection slips, and had 25 jobs in 11 years, before finally emerging as an established and highly-paid author.

It surely says something about staying power, determination and the will to succeed, doesn't it?

THURSDAY — JANUARY 27.

"THERE is nothing, absolutely nothing, half so much worth doing as simply messing about in boats."

I'm sure most of us are familiar with these words from Kenneth Grahame's wonderful book, "The Wind In The Willows", but personally, I'd go even further. I think there is absolutely nothing like "messing about" anywhere to recharge our batteries and give us a sense of well-being.

Whether we choose to potter on the river, in our garden, stroll around town or in the country, we should never feel guilty about taking the time to slow down and simply enjoy life — we live in a world so full of beauty and interest.

FRIDAY — JANUARY 28.

BISHOP Tutu has long been renowned for his wise words and I was particularly impressed by one of his speeches in which he declared, "If the rule of 'An Eye For An Eye' dominated, the whole world would soon be blind."

These words are worth thinking about today and every day.

SATURDAY — JANUARY 29.

I CAME on these lines in a church magazine published in Canada many years ago, and would like to share them with you today:

Good morning, God, and thank you
For the glory of the sun,
And thank you for the health I have
To get my duty done.
I shall pursue my daily art,
Without complaint or fear
And spend my every effort
To be friendly and sincere.
I know there have been many days
That I have whiled away,
But this is one that I will try
To make Your special day.

SUNDAY — JANUARY 30.

HONOUR thy father and thy mother: that thy days may be long upon the land which the Lord thy God giveth thee.   Exodus 20:12

MONDAY — JANUARY 31.

SOME people in business won't waste a minute of their working day. "Time is money," they will tell you. Talking about this one day with Henry, a retired clerk, I found that he thinks exactly the opposite!

"I have a small pension," he said. "It's not much but enough for me to live on. So for me, money is time. It gives me the time to do all the little things I've always wanted."

There goes a contented man.

DEAR GREEN PLACE

February

TUESDAY — FEBRUARY 1.

IT would be true to say that most of us have a favourite song. It can remind us of a particular occasion in our lives, and whenever we hear it, we travel back through the years to recall that special moment.

While some songs may be more memorable than others, it might be argued that a song is just like friendship — if it strikes the right note, it can create so much harmony.

WEDNESDAY — FEBRUARY 2.

HAVE you ever bought an old book and found a handwritten inscription inside? I always appreciate such things for the glimpse of the original owner which they provide.

One example which I was particularly pleased to discover was this little prayer, written in beautiful copperplate script on the flyleaf of a guide to the Lake District:

Dear Lord, please guard me on my way,
Please guide my feet, lest I should stray,
Please give me strength, when storms come near,
To overcome enfeebling fear,
And Lord, I beg, my whole life through
Please let me ever walk with You.

THURSDAY — FEBRUARY 3.

WHEN Betty moved into a smaller house in an unfamiliar town, she was dismayed to find that her possessions now overspilled the space available.

"And so," she said, "in order to get rid of the clutter, I started taking things down to my local charity shop. The volunteers who ran it soon got to know me and, before I knew it, I too had become a regular helper there. It was the best move I ever made — now I have a house empty of clutter, and a life full of friends."

Sounds like a good swap to me, Betty!

FRIDAY — FEBRUARY 4.

SILENT PEACE

WHAT peace there is in silence,
The silence of the hills,
The strength of distant mountains
Can ease our worldly ills.
What peace lies in the forest,
Beneath the oak and beech,
A lesson learned in silence
These ancient trees can teach.

What peace there is in silence,
Such healing in our lives,
This gentle gift of nature
Our quiet hope revives.
What peace lies deep within us
If we will seek and find,
In moments spent in silence
Discover peace of mind.

Iris Hesselden.

SATURDAY — FEBRUARY 5.

DO you like birthdays? Our friend Ruby doesn't, while her sister Alison can't wait to celebrate on the day.

I know many others who find a birthday a great reason for making the most of the occasion. Those who dislike birthdays often say they feel shy about "adding another ring to the trunk".

Whatever your views, a birthday is an important day to mark in your diary, and a time to quote a thought like this:

"A birthday is a time to thank God for life, with all its endless store of great new experiences."

SUNDAY — FEBRUARY 6.

AND the Lord said unto him, Peace be unto thee; fear not: thou shalt not die.

Judges 6:23

MONDAY — FEBRUARY 7.

WHEN Marion was adopted in Vietnam by young friends of ours, she had known only hunger for the first years of her life. A bottle was attached to each of the cots in the orphanage and the little ones who could successfully struggle to reach the teat survived.

The first day after Marion's adoption she was eating a bowl of rice in a restaurant. She concentrated on every mouthful. At one point a single grain dropped to the floor.

The young girl carefully climbed down from her stool and picked up the grain of rice — it was far too precious to waste.

STILL WATERS

TUESDAY — FEBRUARY 8.

IT had been a warm and sunny afternoon, and I'd promised myself a walk, when suddenly I noticed that the blue sky had turned an ominous grey. Moments later the heavens opened in a cloudburst.

The Lady of the House turned to me with a smile. "My goodness, Francis," she said. "That was lucky! If you'd already left home you would have got soaked. Now you can wait indoors until the rain has stopped, and when you do set off the whole world will smell sweet and fresh for you!"

Isn't it strange how the same event can have a positive as well as a negative side?

WEDNESDAY — FEBRUARY 9.

I LIKE stories which reveal that famous people often possess "the common touch". I remember one such tale about a mother who took her eight-year-old son, a lad who showed musical promise, to a recital by the great pianist Paderewski.

As the audience waited for the start of the performance, the boy broke loose from his mother. She was horrified to see him jump on to the platform and sit himself down at the piano, where he started to play "chopsticks"!

At that moment the virtuoso entered. He showed no trace of anger and, leaning over the boy's extended arms, added a set of brilliant variations. The young boy would surely never forget playing that duet! Let's hope it inspired him to work hard at his music lessons — and perhaps other lessons, too.

THURSDAY — FEBRUARY 10.

*T*HANKS. You know, I often find it remarkable just how much difference that one small word can make. For example, I'm always happy to hold open a door or stand aside to let someone else go first, yet it makes me feel so much better if my gesture is acknowledged. In fact, it reminds me of a verse I was taught as a small child:

"Thanks" is such a little word, that sometimes we lose sight
Of making sure we use it just as often as we might.
So next time someone's helpful, make sure you pause to say
A word of recognition — it might make someone's day!

FRIDAY — FEBRUARY 11.

I ONCE read about the Italian Renaissance which left me feeling that, despite all the inherent difficulties and dangers, it must still have been a wonderfully exciting time during which to have lived.

I was particularly struck by the words of one Francesco Guicciardini, a statesman who, even while living in the midst of all that remarkable creativity, was still inspired to observe that there was one thing worth making above all else. He wrote:

"Since there is nothing so well worth having as friends, never lose a chance to make them."

It's rather nice to know that some values never change!

SATURDAY — FEBRUARY 12.

"CHILDREN should be seen and not heard." How often have you come across these words over the years?

We once visited some friends who were delighted to meet up with us again after a long time. After the initial introductions to various young family members we'd not met before, the grown-ups settled down to catch up.

Three-year-old Craig, however, was keen to remain the centre of attention and did his best to show his new friends his favourite toys.

"Be quiet, Craig," his mother told him gently after a while. "People are trying to talk."

The little lad looked up with sad eyes. "But I'm a people, too," he said in his defence.

As we get caught up in the importance of our adult world, let's never forget that children have a right to be heard, because as young Craig so rightly said, they are people, too!

SUNDAY — FEBRUARY 13.

TURN us again, O Lord God of hosts, cause thy face to shine; and we shall be saved.

Psalms 80:19

MONDAY — FEBRUARY 14.

FRIENDS of ours were celebrating their Golden Wedding and remarked that they loved one another just as much as when they first met. This reminded me of a saying by Ursula K. Le Guin:

"Love doesn't sit there like a stone, it has to be made, like bread; remade all the time, made new."

TUESDAY — FEBRUARY 15.

PRAYER FOR THE NIGHT

DEAR Lord, should I wake
*   before it grows light,*
Please let me not brood
*   on the fears of night.*
But let me think back
*   to the joys of the day,*
And dwell on the good things
*   that all came my way.*
Please help me not fret
*   over problems ahead,*
But trust in Your grace
*   and Your goodness instead,*
And when at last darkness
*   gives way to the dawn —*
Then let me rejoice
*   in Your blessed new morn.*

                    Margaret Ingall.

WEDNESDAY — FEBRUARY 16.

DO you ever set out to accomplish something, but then give up because you feel overwhelmed by the sheer difficulty involved? If so, take heart from some words written by the American author and Unitarian clergyman, Edward Everett Hale.

As an influential reformer, he wrote, "I am only one, but I am still one: I cannot do everything, but still I can do something; and because I cannot do everything, I will not refuse to do the something that I can do."

Do you feel ready to try again? I do hope so!

THE FRIENDSHIP BOOK

FOR several years now Stan has acted as secretary to a public speaking club. It's a thriving group and his duties often include making arrangements for speakers to come and address them.

"I certainly get to meet some interesting people," he told me, "and some are well-known faces. But you can never predict just who will be amenable, and who will feel that their celebrity status makes them more important than anyone else. I can't help thinking that it's just as G. K. Chesterton once said: 'The really great person is the person who makes every person feel great'."

We can't all be famous, but that needn't stop us trying to behave like a "really great person"!

FRIENDS of ours stopped outside a little church in the country, far from noise and crowds, and read these simple words:

Where there is pain, may you have peace and mercy. Where there is self-doubting, may you have new confidence.

Where there is tiredness or exhaustion, may you have understanding, patience and renewed strength.

Where there is fear, may you have love and fresh courage.

A place further away from the problems of the world would be hard to imagine but here, isolated from them all, was someone acknowledging everyday stress, and offering a solution.

SATURDAY — FEBRUARY 19.

I CAME across an observation made by the writer Edith Wharton: "There are two ways of spreading light; to be the candle, or the mirror that reflects it."

This struck me as a most perceptive and encouraging remark, for although it is not given to all of us to be an original source of enlightenment or wisdom, we can certainly do our best to be a mirror to such qualities, reflecting and spreading the light around us wherever we go.

SUNDAY — FEBRUARY 20.

THE grace of our Lord Jesus Christ be with your spirit. Amen.   Philemon 1:25

MONDAY — FEBRUARY 21.

I SAW these words prominently displayed in a florist's shop, and wanted to share them with you today:

RECIPE FOR GOOD HEALTH

For attractive lips, speak words of kindness.
For beautiful eyes, look for the good in others.
To lose weight, let go of stress, hatred, anger, discontentment and the need to control others.
For poise, walk with knowledge and self-esteem.
To strengthen your arms, hug at least three people a day.
Touch someone with your love.
To strengthen your heart, forgive yourself — and others.

Have a healthy day!

MEADOW
SWEET

TUESDAY — FEBRUARY 22.

THE Lady of the House and I attended an illustrated talk on the subject of Indonesia. It was given by a man who had spent a great deal of his life visiting other parts of the world, both on and off the beaten track. Afterwards, prompted by the wonderful pictures we had just seen, one woman asked him if he didn't find coming home rather boring.

"Not at all!" he assured her. "You see, when I'm abroad, it's easy to look at everything with curiosity and appreciation, so I simply keep up the habit when I get back. It's not difficult — have a go and you'll see!"

That sounds like excellent advice to me. There is so much of interest and beauty all around us that it's a shame to ignore things simply because they happen to be on our own doorstep.

WEDNESDAY — FEBRUARY 23.

A BUSINESSMAN who is always on the move, in charge of a large pool of employees and commuting regularly from his office to clients in other parts of the country, was asked by a colleague why the letters A.S.A.P. kept appearing in papers on his desk and in his diary,

"Surely," said his associate, "you do everything on your demanding schedule As Soon As Possible. Why do you emphasise it?"

The busy executive smiled. "Everybody keeps getting these four letters wrong," he said. "They don't mean what people think. In my life and book they stand for 'Always Say A Prayer'."

THURSDAY — FEBRUARY 24.

I ONCE read the story of a young clergyman who took the much-loved 23rd Psalm as the subject of a talk to a group of children.

There was a lot they didn't know, he told them. In fact, they were pretty much like sheep themselves and, of course, sheep need a shepherd. He then asked the children who they thought the shepherd was, and after thinking about it for a little while, one lad piped up, "Jesus is the shepherd."

The young minister looked taken aback. "Then who am I?" he asked the child.

"Oh, you're the sheepdog," the boy replied. "There's only one shepherd."

FRIDAY — FEBRUARY 25.

JEAN, one of the best guides-through-life that the Lady of the House and I have ever known, reminded us one day:

"Please count your health instead of your wealth." Then, still in the counting mode, she added:

Count your blessings instead of your crosses.
Count your gains instead of your losses.
Count your joys instead of your woes.
Count your friends instead of your foes.
Count your smiles instead of your tears.
Count your courage instead of your fears.

As Jean left us, we agreed that nobody could have given us a more helpful countdown to happier living, and we started our counting there and then!

SATURDAY — FEBRUARY 26.

OUR neighbour Tom has a wise friend who firmly believes that no problem in life is so difficult that it can't be helped by having a nap.

The novelist John Steinbeck once said that putting a problem aside for a few hours is a good way to solve it. He did this when he was having difficulty thinking up a suitable ending to one of his storylines.

"It's a common experience," he told friends, "that a problem difficult at night is resolved in the morning after the committee of sleep has worked on it."

SUNDAY — FEBRUARY 27.

AND, Thou, Lord, in the beginning hast laid the foundation of the earth; and the heavens are the works of thine hands.   Hebrews 1:10

MONDAY — FEBRUARY 28.

AT a service in a residential home, I was moved to hear that this lovely prayer is used on such occasions:

Lord, we thank Thee for this place in which
    we dwell;
For the love that unites us;
For the peace accorded us this day;
For the hope with which we expect the morrow;
For the health, the work, the food,
And the bright skies that make our lives
    delightful;
For our friends in all parts of the earth,
    and our friendly helpers.

March

THE daffodils in the shopping arcade were on special offer: "Buy two bunches and get one free!" Like many others, the Lady of the House and I were tempted, and bought them.

Arriving home, we decided that they looked rather dejected but hoped that with a little pampering they would improve. So you can imagine our surprise when, by the following morning, they had lifted their heads and were a golden delight.

Aren't we a bit like that ourselves? Sometimes, we are withdrawn and feel dejected, we hang our heads and forget to look up at the trees and the sky. A few words of kindness, however, a friendly smile, and we blossom and grow.

I hope that you, too, will lift up your heads and reach out to the Spring.

LOSING their way, friends came off a busy motorway, and soon found themselves on a quiet side-road where Angus spotted these words on a church notice-board:

"If you're heading in the wrong direction, remember — God allows U-turns."

THURSDAY — MARCH 3.

LIKE most of us I have, on many occasions, been offered various words of advice about getting on with the job in hand and speeding it forward to its completion. Don't we all tend to slow down a little while working on a project?

I recently came across an old Scottish proverb, however, that seems to inspire us to action more than most: "Fools look to tomorrow," it says, "but wise men use tonight."

These words may be as old as the Highland hills, but I'm sure they are well worth sharing today.

FRIDAY — MARCH 4.

A LOCAL history society held an exhibition of Spring customs and folklore. It was a fascinating event and included a display of beautifully-painted eggs, vintage Valentine cards, photographs of pancake races and maypole dancing.

"You know, Francis," the Lady of the House later observed, "I think there must be more customs connected with this time of year than any other season."

I'm sure she's right. Spring, with its daily miracles of beauty and rebirth, is indeed a special time, so it's little wonder that people throughout the ages in many corners of the globe have celebrated it in their own particular way.

I'm always uplifted by the arrival of Springtime, and know that it was equally important to our forebears and will, I'm sure, be just as special to generations yet to come.

THE FRIENDSHIP BOOK

I WAS sorry to see two of my neighbours, both sensible people, arguing over a trivial matter, then refusing to speak to each other for weeks.

Eventually, one of them discovered that she had been wrong in the first place, and wondered if she should own up to her mistake or just keep quiet.

I'm glad to say that after a few days of hard thinking she went to her neighbour and said: "I'm sorry, Jean. You were right and I was wrong."

This situation reminded me of the wise words of Benjamin Disraeli: "One of the hardest things in the world is to admit you are wrong. Nothing is more helpful in resolving a situation than such a frank admission."

D RAW nigh to God and he will draw nigh to you.

James 4:8

I T has been said "life is like March weather, savage and serene in one hour". Yes, life is unpredictable with all its ups and downs, and never ceases to present us with new challenges. It can be trying and exhilarating, sad and surprising, and yet giving great joy and happiness, companionship and love.

Life has indeed what D. H. Lawrence called a "delicate magic". It is a tapestry of many shades and colours.

TUESDAY — MARCH 8.

THIS is a memorable quotation from Mother Teresa to think about today.

She said: "If you are kind, people will accuse you of selfish motives — be kind anyway. If you're successful, you'll win both false friends and true enemies — succeed anyway. What you spend years building, someone may destroy overnight — build anyway.

"The good you do today most people will forget — do good anyway. Give the world the best between you and God; it was never between you and them anyway."

WEDNESDAY — MARCH 9.

ALONG the lane, beneath the trees,
Beside the lake, along the shore,
A glimpse of golden daffodils
And Winter-weary spirits soar.
Beside the busy, noisy road,
Untouched, untroubled, unaware
Of dirt and dust and petrol fumes,
More golden faces, everywhere.

Green now the fields and white the streams,
New life appearing all around,
In budding branches, calling lambs
The Springtime promise can be found.
And though grey clouds may fill the sky,
Or creeping mist obscure the hills,
Through wind and rain or early frost,
You lift our hearts, wild daffodils!

Iris Hesselden.

THURSDAY — MARCH 10.

NEVER get angry with yourself, I was once told, if you suddenly feel envious of someone. Instead, just remind yourself of this thoughtful advice from a Chinese philosopher:

"If you haven't all the things that you want in this world, just be grateful for the things you don't have that you never wanted."

We tend to forget, as the writer Elizabeth O'Connor puts it, that "envy is a symptom of a lack of appreciation of our own uniqueness and self-worth".

Each one of us has something to give that no one else has.

FRIDAY — MARCH 11.

WHEN I called to see our old friend Mary on her birthday, I was surprised to notice that taking pride of place among the cards on her mantelpiece was a small brown Teddy bear. I was soon introduced.

"This is Bruno The Second," she told me. "When I was young I had a knitted teddy I loved dearly, until one day I lost him. He was never found and there's always been a tiny part of me that felt sad about it.

"So, even though she's not a great knitter, my friend Ellen bought some wool and made this one just for me. I think it's one of the nicest presents I've ever been given!"

I know the phrase "money can't buy everything" is often dismissed as a cliché, but doesn't Mary's birthday present show just how true this can be?

SATURDAY — MARCH 12.

THE passage of hundreds of years can be guaranteed to change a great many opinions and ideas, but nevertheless I was interested to chance upon these words of Ailred Of Rievaulx, a Cistercian monk who lived in the twelfth century.

"No medicine is more valuable," he wrote, "none more efficacious, none better suited to the cure of all our temporal ills than a friend, to whom we may turn for consolation in time of trouble, and with whom we may share our happiness in times of joy."

Words which surely prove that the really important things in life never change.

SUNDAY — MARCH 13.

LET us hold fast the profession of our faith without wavering.

Hebrews 10:23

MONDAY — MARCH 14.

TWO hundred executives, at a conference in Columbus, Ohio, were asked to name the quality that makes a person successful.

Eighty per cent listed enthusiasm, saying it is more important than skill, training and even experience. A teacher in a science class used to say that enthusiasm is like the electricity in a battery, the vigour in the air, the warmth in a fire.

"It's the breath in all things alive," he said.

All successful people are enthusiastic about everything they do. Add enthusiasm to your assets and you will be truly unstoppable.

THE FRIENDSHIP BOOK

TUESDAY — MARCH 15.

I LIKE "Wayside Pulpit" messages often seen on posters outside churches. I have to admire the ingenuity displayed in their composition. I was struck by these two examples I noticed one afternoon:

"Get in touch with God by knee mail."

"God knows when you were last in church."

WEDNESDAY — MARCH 16.

I LIKE to think this chair is mine
Where I can sit and feel at peace,
Where trial and trouble fade away
And sorrows cease.
Where I may gently lay my head
And tumble into sleep,
Cradled in your loving arms
And in your valleys deep.
So when I wake I feel refreshed
The world is made anew,
And I go forth with happy heart
And all because of you!

Eva Knights.

THURSDAY — MARCH 17.

JOSEPH was a chiropodist in a small town for over 50 years. He loved his work and once told me why.

"People come into my surgery limping painfully. A few days later I see them in the street looking as if they have wings on their feet."

Not many can say they have helped people to walk on air, but that's what Joseph did!

FRIDAY — MARCH 18.

OVER 250 years ago, a wealthy sea captain, Captain Coram, came on an abandoned infant in a London street. Discovering that little was done for such children, he built a foundling hospital in Bloomsbury and persuaded leading artists and composers to assist in raising money to run it.

Handel gave performances of the Messiah, while Hogarth, Reynolds and Ramsay all gifted pictures.

The hospital no longer exists but a charity, the Coram Family, carries on the good work, helping vulnerable youngsters to find their feet, as the kindly captain did all those years ago.

SATURDAY — MARCH 19.

SMILE!

A SMILE is an investment,
An inner happy glow.
A mood-lifter,
A cheer-giver,
And what do you know?
A smile given can mean
A mirrored smile right back,
A dividend, a brand-new friend,
And a chance for joy to grow.
                    Katy Clarke.

SUNDAY — MARCH 20.

AND when the centurion, which stood over against him, saw that he so cried out, and gave up the ghost, he said, Truly this man was the Son of God.   Mark 15:39

THE FRIENDSHIP BOOK

MONDAY — MARCH 21.

"IT'S a pet hate of mine," confessed Beryl, "when someone asks you how you are, and then doesn't pause long enough to find out. I know people lead busy lives these days, but if you happen to be feeling low, or perhaps even bursting with good news, it's disheartening to find no-one really wants to hear it."

I quite understand what Beryl means, for her comments reminded me of a little rhyme I once came across:

Next time you ask, "How are you?"
Then do make sure you stay
And listen to the answer —
You might make someone's day!

TUESDAY — MARCH 22.

I WAS once having a chat with my friend Harry when he told me about the time he had arranged to have part of his garden path replaced with tarmac.

"There was a little clump of tulip bulbs in one corner and I'd intended to dig them up and replant them somewhere else," he said. "However, they were overlooked and when the workmen arrived they were buried. The next Spring, to my great surprise, I found a tulip poking up through the new path and, do you know, I just hadn't the heart to cut it down and repair the path!

"So there it is to this day, Francis, and it serves as a reminder that if a little tulip can overcome such an obstacle, and survive, then that is an example I should follow."

APPLE
BLOSSOM
TIME

WEDNESDAY — MARCH 23.

A FRIEND who wants to remain anonymous once confided in me: "I wish I were half as great as my wife thinks I am, and only half as stupid as my teenage son thinks I am!"

THURSDAY — MARCH 24.

A YOUNG acquaintance of mine was surfing the Internet when he came on these thoughts by Terri McPherson, who was passing on the hopes and wishes of millions via her webpage:

"I wish you more sunshine than shadows, more comfort than trouble, more grace than greed, more gratitude than need, more days filled with rainbows than rain.

"More joy than money can buy, more love than the heart can hold, more laughter than tears, more courage than fears, more memories than silver or gold."

Words worth echoing around the world.

FRIDAY — MARCH 25.

T HERE is a poem by John Milton which ends: "They also serve who only stand and wait", a line which carries an important message.

It is amazing how often a person can support someone who is troubled, simply by being there. Seeing a friendly, sympathetic face when you are "down in the dumps" can cheer you up hugely. As Easter approaches, there is a supreme example for us to consider — Mary at The Crucifixion.

She signalled that she would stand by Our Lord to the end — and beyond.

SATURDAY — MARCH 26.

A SUNDAY School teacher asked her class if they knew what a miracle was. One little girl put up her hand and said that she had seen one the previous day.

When the slightly-mystified woman asked Emma to tell them all about it, she described how she had witnessed baby chicks hatching out of their eggs when she visited her uncle's farm.

A small miracle maybe, but just one of the many that surround us every day.

SUNDAY — MARCH 27.

H E is not here: for he is risen, as he said. Come, see the place where the Lord lay.

Matthew 28:6

MONDAY — MARCH 28.

S URELY all the essence of Spring with the promise of Summer to come is contained in this verse by Robert Buchanan. You will find it in "White Rose And Red, A Story In Verse".

The fir puts out green fingers,
The pear tree softly blows,
The rose in her dark bower lingers,
But her curtains will soon unclose,
And the lilac will shake her ringlets
Over the blush of the rose.

Born in Glasgow in 1841, Robert was the son of a tailor. He wrote poetry, plays and novels. He left Scotland and went to London, and became well known in his day through his "London Poems".

TUESDAY — MARCH 29.

HERE are some thoughts about being positive and focusing on the months and indeed, years still to come:

"When we fill our hearts with regrets over the failures of yesterday, we have no today in which to be thankful."

"The problem with gazing too frequently into the past is that we may turn around to find that the future has run out on us."

Good thinking! The wise way is to move forward to sample the vitality of both today and tomorrow.

WEDNESDAY — MARCH 30.

THE assistant behind the counter in a small village store was busy selling groceries to a happy, laughing group of customers. I couldn't help but contrast the scene with the rather dull and lifeless picture of shoppers seen the day before in a vast, rather impersonal city supermarket.

Then I caught sight of a sign on the wall behind the assistant. It read:

Friendly shopping is contagious —
Why not start an epidemic?

THURSDAY — MARCH 31.

I ONCE read this saying from Greece: "You don't have to show love in words, because even through the silences, love is clearly heard."

Through the silences . . . Aren't those the moments that we can all use, at meaningful times in our lives, to convey so much?

April

FRIDAY — APRIL 1.

IT'S hard to imagine a better way to usher in the month of April than with this verse from the pen of Harriet Prescott Spofford:

A gust of birdsong, a patter of dew,
A cloud, and a rainbow's warning,
Suddenly, sunshine and perfect blue —
An April day in the morning.

Indeed, what more beautiful sight is there than April raindrops shimmering and sparkling diamond-bright on flower and leaf in Spring sunshine?

Harriet was born in the United States in 1835. A poet and novelist, she was also well known for her short stories, and her other writing for adults and children.

SATURDAY — APRIL 2.

OUR friend Moira had cause to visit an eye specialist and smiled on her return home when she showed the Lady of the House a copy of these words she had read on the wall of the reception area:

"People don't injure their eyesight by looking at the bright side of things."

Now there's a thought for us to remember!

SUNDAY — APRIL 3.

A ND this is the record, that God hath given to us eternal life, and this life is in his Son.

John I 5:11

MONDAY — APRIL 4.

D O you sometimes pass a shop window and suddenly spot the perfect gift for a member of your family or a friend? Irene did so recently when she saw a great little present for her grandson Adam.

She couldn't resist rushing in to buy it, but what intrigued me was how she described the moment.

"It kept winking at me from the window," she said.

What a lovely way to describe how you happen upon the right gift!

TUESDAY — APRIL 5.

H AVE you ever suffered from homesickness? Well, I don't suppose there are many of us who have never experienced such feelings when finding ourselves far from friends and family.

Take heart from the words of Johann Wolfgang von Goethe who once wrote: "To know someone here or there with whom you feel there is understanding, in spite of distances or thoughts unexpressed — that can make of this earth a garden."

It's good to know that however far from our loved ones we may be, the green shoots of love and affection always remain fresh and alive in our hearts.

THE FRIENDSHIP BOOK

SOME say, "All the magic's gone
From this old world of ours",
Have they never seen a rainbow
After April showers?
Have they seen a Winter sunrise,
Thick frost on the trees?
What about wild daffodils
Dancing in the breeze?

Have they missed the Autumn glow
The crunching, golden leaves?
Have they heard the west wind blow
Singing in the eaves?
There is beauty everywhere
If we look around,
And sharing Nature's wonderland,
Magic can be found!

Iris Hesselden.

WE were once saying our au revoirs to a friend leaving for a new life abroad when the Lady of the House said: "You know, I just hate goodbyes. What we all need, today and every day, are more hellos."

Saying hello is certainly a trend to be encouraged. The writer Joseph Liebman said: "Treasure each other in the recognition that we do not know how long we shall have each other."

We hit a more cheerful note when our friend reminded us with a broad smile that every goodbye makes the next hello all the closer.

FRIDAY — APRIL 8.

LIFE for teenagers can be difficult, but how much harder it often is for the parents of teenagers! They face a new and challenging phase in their lives when their children start to reach out for independence.

One friend told us about the struggle she and her husband were having to keep up with their teenage daughter's growing social life, and her circle of friends they often felt they knew little about.

All the same, I couldn't help but be struck by how balanced the parents appeared to be in their approach to this new challenge. They seemed to be very much of the same mind deciding how they were going to tackle things, and when I came across the following quote from Antoine de Saint-Eupery I thought immediately of them:

"Love does not consist in gazing at each other, but looking forward in the same direction."

SATURDAY — APRIL 9.

DIGNITY is a strange and precious gift. You can't see it, you can't touch it, but you always know when someone has it. It is often found amongst the poorest people on God's earth. They may have little else, but if they have dignity they are rich indeed.

Now, a warning: dignity is fragile and has to be treated with the greatest care. Try to stand on it — as some folk do — and you are likely to fall flat on your face!

SUNDAY — APRIL 10.

BUT I trust I shall shortly see thee, and we shall speak face to face. Peace be to thee. Our friends salute thee. Greet the friends by name.

John III 1:14

MONDAY — APRIL 11.

THERE have been many reflections about what we should do after making a mistake, and on how to cope with the doubts that follow. Here — from someone whose name, unfortunately, has not been handed down — is one of the best pieces of advice I have read:

"Mistakes are lessons of wisdom. The past cannot be changed. The future is yet in your power."

TUESDAY — APRIL 12.

OUR friend Dan runs a successful business and reckons that the good results and happy relations with his staff are due to each of his fifty-strong team following these informal rules:

We listen more than we talk.
We smile more than we frown.
We think "we" more than we think "me".
We agree more than we disagree.
We compliment more than we criticise.
We laugh more than we cry.
We do more than we don't.
We act more than we react.
We save more than we squander.
We work more than we whine.

All good maxims for work, and they apply every bit as much to how we live our life at home.

WEDNESDAY — APRIL 13.

THE best appeal for a charity I ever heard was when the speaker, after telling us of the work his organisation did for those in need, added:

"I want you to feel for these people, first in your heart, and then in your pocket."

When the plate was passed round it was filled to the brim.

THURSDAY — APRIL 14.

I ONCE read a story about some American students and found it thought provoking and worth sharing with you today.

A quiet and studious schoolboy was teased, partly because of his bespectacled appearance, but also for his love of books. Things came to a head one day when he was picked on as he was walking home and his books thrown around. A fellow pupil came to his assistance, collected his belongings and walked the rest of the way with him.

From that time on their friendship grew. Time passed as they studied hard at college; then came graduation day. The quiet young man was chosen to give a speech at the ceremony and, as he spoke, it became apparent how desperately unhappy he had been as a schoolboy.

Looking straight at his friend, he said he was so grateful for all the help he had received. He finished with these words: "Never underestimate the power of your actions. With one small gesture you can change a person's life, for better or for worse."

FRIDAY — APRIL 15.

SIR Georg Solti, the famous conductor, was once asked which instrument he thought was the most difficult to play.

He said that in his opinion it must be the second fiddle, as they were certainly the most difficult to recruit. It was usually easy to get first violins, but a second fiddle with great enthusiasm was hard to find.

Then he added a really telling thought: "Most of us find it very difficult to play second fiddle. If, on the other hand, all the second fiddles in an orchestra stopped playing, we would really be well and truly sunk."

SATURDAY — APRIL 16.

CALLING on Sam I found him busy in his potting shed, organising seed trays for his Spring planting. Noticing my doubtful glance at the grey skies outside, he laughed.

"Don't worry, Francis. I'm quite sure that the warmer weather will arrive eventually!"

Watching him, it struck me just how many of the things which enrich our lives are based on such little acts of faith. Whether nurturing plants, planning a coffee morning or a fête, or simply offering the hand of friendship to a stranger, we are showing trust that our efforts will turn out well.

Faith is indeed a strange and unmeasurable quality, but as Samuel Butler once observed, "You can do very little with it, but you can do nothing without it." I second that!

THE FRIENDSHIP BOOK

KEEP yourselves in the love of God, looking for the mercy of our Lord Jesus Christ unto eternal life.

Jude 1:21

I WAS not surprised to read that Princess Anne, a renowned horsewoman, had been seen at an equestrian event, casually looking at items on a stall.

A woman nearby whispered to her four-year-old daughter, "Look, there's the princess!" The little girl then asked loudly, "If she's a princess, where's her crown?"

Without more ado the princess bent down and whispered, "It's in my handbag."

A lovely story, showing a great understanding of a child's sense of wonder.

MANY years ago as a child I was fascinated by a relative's autograph book. It wasn't filled with the names of the rich and famous, but rather with the signatures of Nell's friends. In those days it was the custom to write something inspiring beside your name and among many humorous offerings was this little thought which stood out:

"In your golden chain of friendship, consider me a link."

I'm confident that many of the names written there represented a chain of friendship that lasted a lifetime.

LIFE'S LITTLE JOYS

M AY each little moment of each happy hour,
Add colour to brighten your day,
Like the fragrance surrounding each
favourite flower,
That's frequently drifting your way;
May each little kindness, from those who
are caring,
Be with you wherever you go,
While the joys of new friendships, and
happiness sharing
Help true understanding to grow.

Elizabeth Gozney.

A YOUNG clergyman friend was once telling us about his early working life. One morning, for the first time, he was to conduct a service in a hospital ward of elderly patients, thirty altogether. He was very nervous.

He recalled: "I started walking towards the beds but suddenly felt myself slipping on the polished floor. I lost my balance, fell backwards and skidded several feet along the floor, eventually coming to a stop to a chorus of 'Oohs' from the patients."

On his feet again, he'd said red-faced, "Would someone like to suggest a hymn we can start with?"

"Stand up, stand up for Jesus," suggested a voice from the end bed.

Laugh and the world laughs with you indeed!

FRIDAY — APRIL 22.

ONE day, the weather was so good that Fred couldn't put off preparing his vegetable plot. The job took most of the morning and, as he leaned on his spade, gazing at the finished result he was inclined to wonder for a moment if his efforts were really worth the trouble.

However, he started to think how the garden would look in the height of Summer. He saw in his mind's eye the neat rows of ferny green carrot tops and crisp-leaved lettuces; the tall runner beans and the plump marrows that would grow from the newly-dug earth. And then he remembered a quotation from Eugene Delacroix:

"To feel that you have done what should be done, raises you in your own eyes."

"Despite everything, I definitely felt I had earned the right to stand tall, Francis," he said. "Just as soon as I could straighten my back again, that is!"

SATURDAY — APRIL 23.

HERE is a fine thought to share today from Mother Teresa, who conquered so many problems of her own and has inspired millions:

"I am a little pencil in the hand of a writing God who is sending a love letter to the world."

SUNDAY — APRIL 24.

AND they straightway left their nets, and followed him.
                                                    Matthew 4:20

THE FRIENDSHIP BOOK

<u>MONDAY — APRIL 25.</u>

A NY doctor will tell you that looking on the bright side is good for your health. Yes, I know it's not always easy, and at times it can seem almost impossible. But it is worth persevering.

You don't want to be so busy watching the rain clouds to the west that you don't see the sun breaking through in the east.

<u>TUESDAY — APRIL 26.</u>

I ONCE heard how a rich father in the United States took his son to visit a poor family living on a farm in the country. He wanted to get the boy's views on their lifestyle, so different from his own.

Back in their luxury home, the father asked his son what he thought of the other family's way of life; "Well, Dad, I saw that we have a dog at home, and they have four. We have a pool that reaches to the middle of the garden, and they have a beautiful creek that has no end.

"We have electric lamps in the garden, they have the stars. Our patio reaches to the front yard, they have a whole horizon.

"Thanks, Dad, for letting me see how poor we really are!"

<u>WEDNESDAY — APRIL 27.</u>

H ERE'S a saying to keep in mind today: "Don't tell God you have a big problem. Tell your problem you've got a big God, and you'll scare it away knowing that your big God is with you!"

MIRROR
IMAGE

THURSDAY — APRIL 28.

"HOW many today, Gavin?" I asked when I met him on the street.

"Twenty-six," he grinned. "Two more than yesterday!"

We were talking about blessings. Gavin once told me that, every morning, he counts all the things he has to be glad about. "My blessings," he calls them.

Do you wonder that his is the most cheerful face I meet?

FRIDAY — APRIL 29.

THESE seven words were spotted on a board outside a church in New York:

Seven days, without prayer, makes one weak!

And, at the entrance to a picturesque little kirk near Loch Lomond, in Scotland, were seen another seven words on the same subject:

Life is fragile. Handle it with prayer!

SATURDAY — APRIL 30.

JIM was a farmer all his life. When he retired I asked him what he had learned from his years of hard work.

He replied, "Patience. You can't hurry the crops. The sun will shine when it wants to and the rain won't come till it's good and ready. We all know that nothing can change that."

Yes, there are many things we can leave safely in the hands of Nature. She knows best, for she's been around a long time!

May

BY this we know that we love the children of God, when we love God, and keep his commandments.

John I 5:2

GOOD NEIGHBOURS

THERE is comfort in the knowledge
They're never far away,
Though sometimes they just smile and wave
Or pass the time of day.
But when the storms are raging
Or trouble lies ahead,
I know that I can turn to them,
To smooth the path I tread.

There is comfort in good neighbours,
They're just a call away,
And when they lend a helping hand
They brighten any day.
So don't forget as time slips by
To share a smile or two,
Let others know and understand
You're a good neighbour too.

Iris Hesselden.

THE FRIENDSHIP BOOK

TUESDAY — MAY 3.

LIKE many happily married couples, John and Jane found that they could sometimes have disagreements over trivial matters.

Then a friend shared with them these two good reasons why it is foolish, at any time, to fly into a temper or a tantrum:

Anger is a condition in which the tongue works faster than the mind.

For every minute in which you are angry with someone, you lose sixty seconds of happiness that you will never get back.

WEDNESDAY — MAY 4.

IN spite of the tragedies of the Brontë family's life, Charlotte Brontë never lost her Christian faith. These words are penned in her Yorkshire novel "Shirley", linked with the experience of Shirley's friend Caroline Helstone:

"Most people have a period or periods in their lives when they have felt forsaken when, having long hoped against hope and still seen the day of fruition deferred, their hearts have truly sickened within them. This is a terrible hour, but it is often the darkest part which proceeds the rise of day: that turn of the year when January wind carries over the waste at once the dirge of departing Winter and the prophecy of coming Spring.

"Yet, let whoever grieves still cling first to love and faith in God. God will never deceive, never finally desert him. 'Whom He loveth, He Chasteneth'. The words are true and should not be forgotten."

BRIGHT OUTLOOK

THURSDAY — MAY 5.

THE Lady of the House's friend, Iris, takes a few minutes every so often to jot down the things she has achieved. It brings her a great sense of inspiration to do more, she finds.

Helen Hayes, the distinguished American actress, said that her mother always drew a distinction between achievement and success. Achievement, according to Helen's mother, is the knowledge that you have studied, worked hard and done the best that is in you. Success is being praised by others.

Winning honours is fine but not as satisfying as personal achievement. Setting a long or short-term goal and working hard until you accomplish it takes motivation.

FRIDAY — MAY 6.

WHEN I went to visit Steve I found him in his garden, planting a sapling. "This is to replace my old apple tree," he explained. "It blew down last year in the gales, and we do miss it.

"Every Spring it gave us beautiful blossom, and every Autumn it produced lots of crisp and delicious fruit. But it wasn't until it had gone that we realised how important it was to us."

Steve's words set me thinking, for just how often is it that we take the good, undemanding parts of our life for granted, and concentrate only on the irritating, unsatisfactory things? In future, why not try to be a bit more appreciative of the important things in life — whether they are people or apple trees!

SATURDAY — MAY 7.

WHEN the Lady of the House and I go out and about we always try, whenever possible, to call at a local church to have a few moments of quiet contemplation to help us on our way.

Once, in the ancient city of Durham, we had the opportunity to visit the magnificent cathedral. We found these words in a hymn book and I'd like to share them with you today:

In Christ there is no east or west,
In Him no north or south,
But one great fellowship of love,
Throughout the whole wide earth.

Wonderful words that can be read in a moment and last a lifetime!

SUNDAY — MAY 8.

THE Lord preserveth the strangers; he relieveth the fatherless and widow: but the way of the wicked he turneth upside down.

Psalms 146:9

MONDAY — MAY 9.

HERE is an unusual notice which a friend saw on a church notice board:

You are requested not to make use of the world's greatest labour-saving device. It is freely available and is known by its favourite name — *Tomorrow.*

Now, isn't that the kind of request that can do wonders no matter where we are? At home as well as when we are out and about.

TUESDAY — MAY 10.

OVER thirty years ago Mary Davidson of Edinburgh wanted to raise money for Christian Aid. She set up a trestle table outside St Andrew's and St George's Church and piled it high with second-hand books. It was an instant success. The following year she and her friends put out more tables.

Since then the annual book sale has grown into Britain's biggest single fundraising event during Christian Aid Week. Every day the church and pavement outside are crammed with tables laden with books of all kinds.

It's astonishing what you can do if you try, isn't it?

WEDNESDAY — MAY 11.

TALKING with a few friends about the disciplines of an earlier generation one day, someone said: "Tidiness meant so much. I remember our grandmother's rule was — 'A place for everything, and everything in its place'."

At this, the youngest there, a 27-year-old, not long promoted to a section manager's post in his firm, reminded us that some old ideas still apply in today's world. He quoted this notice which is prominently displayed in his busy workplace:

If you open it, close it.
If you turn it on, turn it off.
If you unlock it, lock it up.
If you break it, admit it.
If you borrow it, return it.
If you move it, put it back.
If you make a mess, clean it up.

THURSDAY — MAY 12.

WEATHER WATCH

LIFE'S like a weather forecast,
And if we look around,
Many strange examples
Of this likeness can be found.

Temperatures can often rise
In certain situations,
And storm clouds tend to gather
In cantankerous locations.

A fog of sheer frustration
Cannot be classed as funny,
But when it clears, by thunder,
The outlook can be sunny.

Frosty implications
That events are sometimes showing,
Are not so chilly if we know
Which way the wind is blowing.

J. M. Robertson.

FRIDAY — MAY 13.

THE new clergyman wanted to make some changes. They were not big but some people were displeased. A meeting was called and one parishioner after another said, "But we have always done it this way!"

At last an elderly man stood up and said quietly, "It used to be ritualism that held up progress in the church; now it's rut-ualism."

That jolted them. They agreed to give the changes a chance — and now they like them!

SATURDAY — MAY 14.

ISN'T it strange how, in spite of all the labour-saving devices which we have in our homes nowadays, we somehow seem to have less time on our hands? A friend was saying how sorry he was to have missed seeing a highly-recommended play at the theatre.

"I just couldn't seem to find the time!" he told me.

But the truth is that time isn't found lying around. Like most of the things we deem worthwhile in life — good friends, good books and good food, for example — finding time takes effort.

As Charles Buxton once said, "You will never find time for anything. You must make it."

SUNDAY — MAY 15.

PRAY for us: for we trust we have a good conscience, in all things willing to live honestly.   Hebrews 13:18

MONDAY — MAY 16.

DO words count more than actions? This tends to form the basis of an ongoing discussion whenever I meet up with a few friends for an hour of interesting chat and good-natured verbal cut-and-thrust.

I think the best point at one of our recent meetings was made when someone quoted these words:

"People may doubt what you say, but they will always believe what you do."

THE FRIENDSHIP BOOK

TUESDAY — MAY 17.

I THOUGHT I would pass on to you what our usually cheerful friend John said to me.

"You know, my road has been all uphill recently, just one thing after another with nothing really to smile about. I have been feeling quite down in the dumps. But I have found a wonderful pick-me-up, a large bottle labelled 'Forgetting Yourself'.

"Take one large spoonful as often as required, it says. It seems to be doing me good!"

WEDNESDAY — MAY 18.

THE Lady of the House looked up from the biography she was reading, and smiled at me. "Here's a riddle for you," she said. "What is it that the more you spend, the more of it remains?"

I couldn't guess, so she enlightened me. "Cheerfulness is the answer! But it wasn't really a proper riddle — it's just a quotation from Ralph Waldo Emerson. I do like it, though, don't you?"

I do indeed, and will make a resolution to be as profligate with cheerfulness as possible.

THURSDAY — MAY 19.

WE don't go to the optician's seeking good advice for living rather than seeing. But a friend who went for his regular eye test was intrigued to read this thought, printed in large letters on the wall:

"Your eyes are placed in front for one good reason. It is more important to look ahead than to look back."

Sound advice, don't you agree?

FRIDAY — MAY 20.

GEOFF is an authority on hymns. He has been an organist for years and can tell many a tale about the verses and their authors. We were talking one day when I mentioned an old hymn I had not heard for some time, written by Norman Macleod in the 19th century. It starts:

Courage brother, do not stumble, though thy path be dark as night.

Geoff replied, "Oh, yes, I remember it well from my schooldays. We had an annual cross-country race and at morning assembly, the headmaster, who had a good sense of humour, always announced it as the hymn for that morning."

SATURDAY — MAY 21.

ON Broadway, New York's famous theatre entertainment area, they call applause "hand-to-hand" music. Now, isn't that a delightful description? Applause or hand-clapping is like music to the ears of performers eager to hear a favourable reaction to their performance on stage.

I suggest that, depending on circumstances, when a person outwith showbusiness has done a good piece of work, we should take a lesson from theatre audiences and offer an inspiring burst of hand-clapping.

SUNDAY — MAY 22.

AND when I saw him, I fell at his feet as dead. And he laid his right hand upon me, saying unto me, Fear not; I am the first and the last.

Revelation 1:17

MONDAY — MAY 23.

AS a wise friend used to say, "You can't be all things to all people, and you can't do all things at once. What's more, you can't do all things equally well, and you can't do all things better than everyone else."

We are all — there's the word again! — human. The answer is to find out who we are, and to be ourselves.

TUESDAY — MAY 24.

ONE of the best thoughts I have read about friendship is this from Oprah Winfrey:

"Lots of people want to ride with you in the limousine, but what you want is someone who will take the bus with you when the limousine breaks down."

WEDNESDAY — MAY 25.

EDITH Cavell was an accomplished woman, a talented artist, linguist and teacher; yet it was not until her father became ill that she discovered her true vocation — that of nursing.

Sadly, it was this desire to save lives that led her to her demise, for whilst running a training school for nurses in Belgium during the Great War she was sentenced to death for aiding Allied soldiers to escape. Yet she did not regret her impulse to help her fellow men. "Patriotism is not enough. I have no hatred or bitterness towards anyone," she said just before her execution.

Now if only that way of thinking was a little more widespread then we might indeed, in the words of the song, "heal the world".

THE FRIENDSHIP BOOK

THURSDAY — MAY 26.

AMONG the passions the Lady of the House and I share is a love of horticulture. Each year we watch with delight on television the famous Chelsea Flower Show.

I like the story that one year an enterprising blackbird built its nest in one of the gardens there and went on to sit on a clutch of eggs. Now, there is a rule that at the end of the show all exhibits are promptly cleared away but, showing great compassion, the authorities decided that the garden with the precious nest must be left undisturbed until the eggs were hatched and the fledgling birds had flown.

It is heart-warming to read of this respect for nature and God's creations.

FRIDAY — MAY 27.

AMONGST the famous poems of the seventeenth century is one written by Rev. George Herbert, "The Pulley":

When God at first made man,
Having a glass of blessings standing by;
"Let us," said He, "Pour on him all we can . . ."

Still as apt a wish today, surely, as in those far-off times.

SATURDAY — MAY 28.

CONSIDER the postage stamp: its usefulness consists in the ability to stick to one thing till it gets there.

Josh Billings.

PERFECT PAL

THE FRIENDSHIP BOOK

SUNDAY — MAY 29.

PRAISE the Lord; for the Lord is good: sing praises unto his name; for it is pleasant.

Psalms 135:3

MONDAY — MAY 30.

I BUMPED into Davina one afternoon and found her buzzing with enthusiasm about a computer lesson she had just received from her niece. I was not too surprised for, despite her mature years, Davina has never allowed anything to discourage her interest in the changing world around her.

"You see," she explained as I was admiring her eagerness to learn, "when I was a small child and struggling with some of my lessons, my grandfather used to encourage me by quoting an old saying: 'Be not afraid of growing slowly; be only afraid of standing still.' It has stood me in good stead throughout my life."

I like that message — like Davina, I believe it's never too late for any of us!

TUESDAY — MAY 31.

*G*OD *be with you in the morning,*
  Guide and bless you through the day,
Fill you with His love and comfort,
  Bring you strength along your way.
God be with you, when the sunshine
  Like true friendship glows so bright,
And when stars and moon shine gently,
  God be with you through the night.

Elizabeth Gozney.

June

OUR JOURNEY

THIS is the journey and this is the road,
Helping each other and sharing the load,
Walking together and seeking the way,
Sharing the wonder and seizing the day.

Making discoveries, lessons to learn,
New exploration as seasons return,
Finding a way to forget and forgive,
Counting our blessings and learning to live.

This is the journey and now is the time,
New paths to follow and mountains to climb,
Travelling onward, enjoying each mile,
Rejoice in the moment, the journey worthwhile.

Iris Hesselden.

WHILE we can all appreciate the advantages of early rising, especially during the brighter and longer days of Spring and Summer, I don't think the sentiment has ever been expressed better than in the memorable words of Benjamin Franklin:

"The morning hour has gold in its mouth."

Make sure you don't miss it.

THE FRIENDSHIP BOOK

FRIDAY — JUNE 3.

I HAVE been dipping once more into Great-Aunt Louisa's diaries. Each year in company with cousins, Louisa, a talented artist and book illustrator, visited the continent to sketch and paint. An entry for a long-ago Summer reads:

"*June 3rd* — Home again! I have painted beautiful old churches, flower markets, canal-side houses and many other things.

"Next week sees the wedding of James and Katherine. I wish them every joy. I hope their marriage will be rich in mutual love and support. This year when in Brussels, we heard of a lovely wedding custom. On their wedding day Belgian brides carry a handkerchief embroidered with their name. Afterwards, the handkerchief is framed and hung in the bride's new home. There it remains until the next wedding in the family, when the new bride's name is embroidered on it.

"A happy and enduring marriage is surely one of life's blessings," observes Louisa. A tiny bouquet of painted roses ends the diary entry.

SATURDAY — JUNE 4.

HERE are some wise words from the pen of the writer Ralph Waldo Emerson:

"Finish each day and be done with it. You have done what you could. Some blunders and absurdities no doubt crept in; forget them as soon as you can.

"Tomorrow is a new day; begin it well and serenely and with too high a spirit to be encumbered by your old nonsense."

THE FRIENDSHIP BOOK

SUNDAY — JUNE 5.

BUT if we walk in the light, as he is in the light, we have fellowship one with another, and the blood of Jesus Christ his Son cleanseth us from all sin.

John I 1:7

MONDAY — JUNE 6.

I CAME across these thought-provoking quotations in a church magazine entitled "Life's Little Instructions":

Always accept an outstretched hand.
Look people in the eye.
Be the first to say "Hello".
Make new friends but always cherish old ones.

The Good Book urges us to be a good neighbour. We'll certainly do well if we keep these rules in mind every day!

TUESDAY — JUNE 7.

THE mantelpiece holds many a card or souvenir. Sometimes it's a postcard from a friend on holiday, or it can be a tiny ornament, a souvenir from a happy time gone by.

A friend pointed out an unusual item, a piece of folded cardboard with the letters "T.T.T.". I opened it to reveal these lines:

Put it in a place
Where it's easy to see —
This cryptic admonishment T.T.T.
So whenever depressingly low you climb,
It's well to remember that
THINGS TAKE TIME.

QUIET CORNER

WEDNESDAY — JUNE 8.

OUR friend Kirsty was telling us how her day had turned out "spellbindingly beautiful" and she felt it would be a shame not to share it with us across the miles. She wrote:

"Tonight's sunset was in pastel shades of the most delicate lilacs and pinks. The occasional misty floating cloud was tinged with purple hues, blending to perfection with the colour of the distant hills.

"As darkness fell, the sky changed to a subtle shade of dove grey, brilliantly illuminated by a full moon. If a fairy had fluttered by, I would not have been surprised.

"It is now a clear, cloudless moonlit night, the blackbirds have finished their song and gone to bed. I will sit here for a while and watch the stars twinkle into view."

Isn't it good to take time out at the end of another busy day and let our eyes drift heavenwards?

THURSDAY — JUNE 9.

IT is wise to look closely at our attitude to the people we meet as well as to friends and family.

A student of human nature once said: "Attitude is the key to success or failure in almost all of life's endeavours."

It determines how we are interacting at any given moment, not only with other people but also with ourselves.

Have a Good Attitude Day!

FRIDAY — JUNE 10.

*WHEN the lark sings
He takes the strings
Of my heart,
Lifts them
To the very edge of Heaven.
In the fiddle of his notes
The skill of all the symphonies
That ever were.
In one voice
The grace of God.*

Kenneth C. Steven.

SATURDAY — JUNE 11.

THE eldest of six lively children and a close friend and helper to her mother, 17-year-old Sarah left home to go to university 300 miles away. Many were the tears shed the night before she set off, but Sarah was determined.

"It won't be easy leaving the security of home," she told her friend Pam before she left, "but somehow I'll do it. I'm determined to pursue my studies, and there's so much I want to do with my life."

Her youthful energy reminded me of some words I once read: "Man cannot discover new oceans unless he has the courage to lose sight of the shore."

SUNDAY — JUNE 12.

GRACE and peace be multiplied unto you through the knowledge of God, and of Jesus our Lord.   Peter II 1:2

MONDAY — JUNE 13.

"EVERY now and again take a good look at something not made with hands — a mountain, a star, the curve of a stream. There will come to you wisdom and patience and solace and, above all, the assurance that you are not alone in the world."

That was said by Sidney Lovett, one-time chaplain of Yale University. He must, I'm sure, have been much valued there, for even today such words continue to uplift and inspire all those who hear them.

TUESDAY — JUNE 14.

ARE you the sort of person who is full of different enthusiasms? It can certainly be an attractive trait, but is perhaps even better if matched by dedication.

Ian was a man whose house bore testament to the wide range but short-lived nature of his interests, for it was full of do-it-yourself jobs never quite completed, walking boots hardly worn, a box of watercolours abandoned after only a few half-hearted attempts at painting.

Ian's wife loved his eagerness to try new things, but wished it could be matched by patience and resolve. However, rather than say anything too discouraging, she sewed a cross-stitch sampler to hang above his desk, with words written by Longfellow: "Great is the art of beginning, but greater is the art of ending."

A good way of recommending perseverance. I do hope it worked!

THE FRIENDSHIP BOOK

WEDNESDAY — JUNE 15.

"EAST, west — home's best" is still one of the best-known sayings in the world.

How true! When things go wrong and you are far from family, friends and home, isn't it nearly always back to the fold that we go? In fact, the word "home" conjures up thoughts of all things heartwarming and inspiring, such as words of sympathy, the warmth of a welcome back and, above all, family and loyal friends.

I think the writer Vernon G. Baker put it well with these words: "Where is our home? Home is where the heart can laugh without shyness, home is where the tears of every heart can dry at their own pace."

THURSDAY — JUNE 16.

THE Lady of the House had been talking on the telephone to an old neighbour of ours, who had just moved house. She put down the receiver thoughtfully.

"It's funny," she observed, "that when folk talk about meeting new people, I sometimes picture how it would be if you could make friends just as if you were making a cake. I wonder what qualities we would mix in — a generous helping of loyalty, a dash of humour, a sprinkling of frankness, but not too much . . .?"

I had to smile at the vision conjured up, but on the whole I'm not sure such precision of choice would be a good thing. I think I prefer things the way they are now, and if that includes a taste of the unexpected, then so much the better!

FRIDAY — JUNE 17.

OF course things happen which annoy us from time to time. But if we are sensible we soon learn that bad temper never pays.

Someone once said that anger blows out the lamp of the mind, while another writer described it as "a short madness".

A third unknown writer advised, "Never answer an angry word with an angry word. It's the second remark that starts the trouble."

The best advice is still the simplest — count up to ten . . . !

SATURDAY — JUNE 18.

EACH June the inhabitants of Dumfries, in the south-west of Scotland, keep a special day to celebrate the fact that their town is secure.

Horsemen ride in procession round its boundaries in an ancient ceremony known as The Riding Of The Marches, and a talented lass from the town is crowned as Queen Of The South.

The day is known as Guid Nychburris Day (Good Neighbours Day), and this spirit of friendliness is reflected as the residents publicly recognise the value of being just that. Few things influence the quality of life so much as community spirit, whether we live in a small village, a busy town or a large city.

SUNDAY — JUNE 19.

AND then shall they see the Son of man coming in the clouds with great power and glory.
                                                        Mark 13:26

MONDAY — JUNE 20.

I ALWAYS admire those people who go through life quietly doing their best to ensure the well-being of others; never making a fuss about their efforts, but simply doing what they can to make the world a better place. I was pleased to come across these words by the writer Thomas Carlyle:

"The work an unknown good man has done is like a vein of water flowing hidden underground, secretly making the ground green."

It's a wonderful description — and one to inspire each one of us to make our own little patch of the earth a lovelier, more fruitful place.

TUESDAY — JUNE 21.

THINK of this picture of perfect peace — a small bird perched on a slender branch overhanging a roaring waterfall. The bird has no cause to be afraid because it puts its trust in the fact that it has been blessed with wings and can take flight to freedom at any time.

We, too, can have perfect peace if we put our trust in the one Lord who protects, guides and leads us and who loves us with a love that is enduring and unfailing. No matter how delicate our situation, no matter how storms rage all around us, we can have that inner peace. If we have worries we should share them with Him so that we are not feeling alone, burdened down with a load of care.

"On Christ the solid rock I stand, all other ground is shifting sand."

WEDNESDAY — JUNE 22.

IT had been a very trying week for the young family. Their washing machine had sprung a leak, the car had broken down and Dad had to struggle with it in the pouring rain. Eight-year-old Mark came home from school after a nasty playground fall, and his sister Susan, aged six, returned with her blouse covered in paint and glue!

Tempers were a little frayed and, by Friday night, everyone was feeling tired and fed up. Mum got up on Saturday morning determined that the weekend would be better. The sun was shining and with a little coaxing, she organised a picnic and they all headed out into the country.

The day was a great success and compensation for the week's frustations. It also helped everyone to face the coming week more cheerfully. I was reminded of the words of George Bernard Shaw: "Life isn't meant to be easy, my child, but take courage, it can be delightful."

How much we all appreciate the good times after the bad!

THURSDAY — JUNE 23.

JOSEPH Addison (1672-1719), the English writer who became Secretary of State in 1717, well knew the value of friendship when he admitted:

"Talking with a friend is nothing else but thinking aloud."

And all these years later, the same still holds good today.

FRIDAY — JUNE 24.

MY HALO

I POLISHED *up my halo*
  As brightly as I could,
I wanted folks to see it
And know that I was good.
Yet quickly did I notice,
And very odd it seemed —
The harder that I polished,
The duller that it gleamed.
So giving up my effort,
For pointless seemed my zest,
I put away my halo
And simply did my best.
But stranger still to tell you,
Since putting it away,
I've noticed that my halo
Shines brighter every day!

Margaret Ingall.

SATURDAY — JUNE 25.

DOES life sometimes seem complicated to you these days? I know we all agree how much new technology can achieve, but things can, on occasion, appear rather confusing and involved.

Sir Winston Churchill once summed it up thus: "All the great things are simple, and many can be expressed in a single word: freedom; justice; honour; duty; mercy; hope."

He was right. These are the important things in life, along with love and kindness. Let us make life as simple as possible.

SUNDAY — JUNE 26.

HEAVEN and earth shall pass away, but my words shall not pass away.

Matthew 24:35

MONDAY — JUNE 27.

HENRY Drummond, the 19th-century writer and lecturer, is perhaps best known for his little book "The Greatest Thing In The World".

It contains this bon mot: "Half the world is on the wrong scent in the pursuit of happiness. They think it consists in having and getting, and in being served by others. It consists in giving, and serving others . . . He that would be happy, let him remember that there is but one way — it is more blessed, it is more happy, to give than to receive."

A familiar sentiment well put!

TUESDAY — JUNE 28.

IT never ceases to amaze and delight me how the faces of old people grow more beautiful with the passing years. The American poet, Karle Wilson Baker, was aware of this when she wrote:

Let me grow lovely, growing old —
So many fine things do;
Laces, and ivory, and gold,
And silks need not be new.

And there is beauty in old trees,
Old streets a glamour hold;
Why may not I, as well as these,
Grow lovely, growing old?

WEDNESDAY — JUNE 29.

IT'S a five-letter word that we hear, today and every day, on everybody's lips, but here are eight thoughts about it that I want to share with you today:

It can buy a house — but not a home.
It can buy a bed — but not sleep.
It can buy a clock — but not time.
It can buy a book — but not knowledge.
It can buy a position — but not health.
It can buy blood — but not life.
It can buy much else — but not love.
Money, you see, isn't everything!

THURSDAY — JUNE 30.

"LET'S call and see our old friend," suggested the Lady of the House as we were passing Phyllis' cottage one day. We received the usual friendly welcome.

"I see you've been reading," I remarked, glancing at a book she had put down. "Some improving literature, no doubt."

"Of course," she replied, smiling. "As a matter of fact, it's an old friend —'Alice In Wonderland'! It isn't childish, you know, to re-read your old favourites and you often find great lessons for adults in children's books.

"I was reading about Pooh Bear the other day, always full of enthusiasm for life, telling friends who could think of nothing to do, 'Let's go out and wish everyone a Happy Thursday!'"

We, too, can try to do something today to make the world a happier place.

July

L IKE most folk, our friends Sally and Adrian go on holiday heavily-laden but there's a difference — not for them designer fashions and the social high life.

Instead, their bags are crammed with outgrown clothes to be given away wherever they see a need. On a recent trip to Calcutta, several bulging suitcases went with them in what has become their way of ensuring that holidays also serve a practical purpose.

M AKE a little time for God
As you're rushing through the day,
Make a little time for Him,
He will help you on your way.

Make a little time to care
In the midst of all you do,
Sending many healing thoughts
To people needing you.

Make a little time for God,
Just a little time to pray,
Care about your fellow man,
You can make a better day!

Iris Hesselden.

SUNDAY — JULY 3.

FOR mine eyes have seen thy salvation, Which thou hast prepared before the face of all people.

Luke 2:30-1

MONDAY — JULY 4.

OUR friend Graeme knows many roads like the back of his hand — after all, he travels thousands of miles each year in the course of his job as a sales director.

I asked him about the different types of road that he travels on, from modern motorways to country roads, even to streets with the speed-reducing humps known as "sleeping policemen".

"You know, Francis," Graeme mused, "travelling along all these roads and highways is not at all unlike the journeys we make in life. The disappointments we encounter are just like these road humps; they slow you down but then you enjoy the smooth stretches that come next."

Words to remember, I'm sure, as we travel the highways and byways of life.

TUESDAY — JULY 5.

I ONCE came across this old Irish proverb, and would like to share it with you today:

"There are many types of ships — wooden ships, plastic ships and metal ships, but the best and most important kind of ships are friendships."

When I quoted it to the Lady of the House, she said: "And remember this, too. The only unsinkable ship in the world is the *friend* ship."

WEDNESDAY — JULY 6.

I LIKE the word "discussion". Being so occupied with the English language and its rich vocabulary, I'm always looking out for words which particularly appeal.

"Discussion" suggests, to me, people getting together to sort out difficulties, as we should all be prepared to do, and reminds me of wise words I once read:

Small minds discuss people,
Average minds discuss events,
Great minds discuss ideas.

There's nothing like talking things over, is there? What a lot of misunderstanding can be avoided by good communication.

THURSDAY — JULY 7.

HAVE you heard of George Muller of Bristol? It won't be surprising if your answer is no, because although he founded orphanages he refused all publicity for the good works he did. He insisted that all the finance and help for his homes must come in answer to prayer.

A typical event was the morning there was no milk for the orphans' breakfast. The children were sitting despondently at their tables when suddenly, there came a knock at the door.

Muller opened it and there stood a milkman. A wheel had come off his cart and he wanted to unload the milk. Could Mr Muller find a use for it?

Little wonder that, when Muller died in 1898, Bristol was a city in mourning.

THE FRIENDSHIP BOOK

FRIDAY — JULY 8.

A FRIEND once made a remark which has stayed with me. I'm not even sure if it was original, but these are the words she used:

"We're as young as yesterday, aren't we?"

What a lovely thought! It's as though today is a new beginning and we are all ready to start afresh. The storms or heavy rain of the previous day are forgotten and we remember only the sunshine.

We have a friend who is now eighty-seven years young who tells us she is still twenty-one inside. And why not? Perhaps the body won't move as quickly as it used to and maybe it's harder to get up in the morning. Don't worry.

If you keep your sense of humour and your optimism, then you're only as old as you feel.

SATURDAY — JULY 9.

IT had been quite a while since I'd bumped into Norman, so I was pleased to see him looking so well and relaxed. I told him so, and he grinned.

"It's all thanks to a present I was given," he explained. "For months I'd been so occupied with work that I hadn't had time for anything else. Then my daughter bought me a rose bush, to which she attached a little message: 'No-one is too busy to smell a rose.'

"It was affectionately meant, but those words certainly made me think. These days, whatever the pressures of business, I always ensure I make time to enjoy the world outside the office."

I like that gentle reminder. Let's try to smell as many roses as we possibly can!

SUNDAY — JULY 10.

FOR of him, and through him, and to him, are all things: to whom be glory for ever. Amen.

Romans 11:36

MONDAY — JULY 11.

WHEN Paula's father was given promotion it meant uprooting the whole family to a town many miles away. At first Paula was greatly upset at the thought of leaving her friends behind but, with encouragement from her mother, resolved to be as brave as possible.

She found a scrapbook, and stuck in photos of all her schoolfriends, along with the addresses and phone numbers that would help her keep in touch. However, when she had finished, there were still several pages left unused.

"Aren't you going to fill the whole book?" asked her mother.

"Oh, no," said Paula. "I must leave room for some new friends as well."

With an attitude like that, I'm sure she will soon be making a great many!

TUESDAY — JULY 12.

AN American thinker, Harry Emerson Fosdick, born in 1878, put it neatly when he said that the world, even then, was moving so fast "that the man who says it can't be done is generally interrupted by someone doing it".

Now, isn't that a wise thought for all who are doing things today? Or planning to do things?

Let's just get on with it!

WEDNESDAY — JULY 13.

OUR friend, Ella, once said: "If someone asks you to walk a mile, you should add an extra mile to your journey. Always do more than you are asked to do."

She is the sort of person who, when she starts something, not only completes it but also delivers more than she is asked for. Ella has coined a word to describe herself. "I'm a finisher," she announces, proudly.

Let's salute all the friends we know like Ella who do that bit more and never quit.

THURSDAY — JULY 14.

WE had invited Sandra and Kenny to afternoon tea, and after their departure the Lady of the House was left glowing by their enthusiastic praise of her baking skills.

Her pleasure made me ponder for a moment on the sometimes underrated importance of a compliment. A few words of genuine appreciation require so little effort and can often make an enormous difference to the person who hears them. Such words can inspire confidence, lift the spirits, perhaps even be the deciding factor as to whether or not someone chooses to persevere rather than give up.

I don't suppose many of us would go quite so far as writer Mark Twain, who claimed that he could "live for two months on a good compliment", but nevertheless, next time you're tempted to say something nice, don't think twice — go ahead and do it!

FRIDAY — JULY 15.

I THINK most of you know that I collect sayings and quotes. Now and then I discover a new one such as this gem. Perhaps it isn't new to you, but I'm sure you'll agree that the words are thought provoking and worth reconsidering:

"He who has health has hope and he who has hope has everything."

Once again, we are reminded how fortunate we are if we are well. Perhaps we have an assortment of minor aches and pains but nothing too serious, nothing to stop us looking forward with hope.

With that precious commodity called hope we can face tomorrow and whatever it may hold.

SATURDAY — JULY 16.

THE HELPER

NOTHING'S too much trouble
As he moves about the place
With an earnest dedication,
That shows clearly on his face.

He's so enthusiastic
In the things he's asked to do.
Complaints are non-existent
As his eagerness shines through.

Although he's only five years old,
To him the cause is just,
For helping his old grandad
In the garden is a must!

J.M. Robertson.

BUILT TO LAST

SUNDAY — JULY 17.

REMEMBER the sabbath day, to keep it holy.

Exodus 20:8

MONDAY — JULY 18.

WHEN visiting a garden centre one afternoon, a friend saw these words on a wall plaque:

The Lord is our Head Gardener. He shows us where to plant the seeds of kindness and gives us the power to help them to grow in strength. If you want the seeds, you can find them in your heart. Plant some today for early flowering!

TUESDAY — JULY 19.

ANNIE didn't have a good start in life. She came from an impoverished and troubled background and, by her own admission, grew into a difficult young woman, suspicious not only of others, but even of her own abilities.

Then she came across the words of Eleanor Roosevelt: "Friendship with oneself is all-important because without it one cannot be friends with anyone else in the world."

That idea really struck home and, as Annie gradually learned to accept herself, she became more generous and understanding to those around her. Nowadays she works with disadvantaged teenagers, and often finds herself passing on this advice.

Isn't it amazing how such a simple seed of awareness can take root and grow into such a fruitful tree?

WEDNESDAY — JULY 20.

I CAME across these words attributed to comedienne Gilda Radner, and feel they sum up perfectly what she called "the delicious ambiguity" of life:

"I wanted a perfect ending . . . Now I've learned the hard way that some poems don't rhyme, and some stories don't have a clear beginning, middle and end. Life is about not knowing, having to change, taking the moment, and making the best of it, without knowing what's going to happen next."

THURSDAY — JULY 21.

H ERE are a few words to remember as we go about our daily lives:

"Not a day passes over the earth but men and women of no note do great deeds, say great words, and suffer noble sorrows."

These are the words of Charles Reade, a Victorian writer, born in 1814 at Ipsden in Oxfordshire, the writer of "The Cloister And The Hearth".

FRIDAY — JULY 22.

I T has been said by more than one person that the reason so many of us never stop searching for happiness, is that we don't, in fact, realise it has already found us.

And how does it do that, you may wonder? The best explanation I have heard is that it comes through doors and windows we did not even know we opened.

SATURDAY — JULY 23.

FIRST LIGHT

THE shadows melted from the cliff
Before the rising sun.
The hills loomed new and strange, as if
The world had just begun.

Bright mountain flowers of every hue
By sparkling dews were kissed,
And everything seemed born anew
In some primeval mist!

Such harmony of tree and flower,
Such majesty profound —
I felt, in that immortal hour,
I walked on holy ground.

Brenda G. Macrow.

SUNDAY — JULY 24.

PREPARE ye the way of the Lord, make straight in the desert a highway for our God.

Isaiah 40:3

MONDAY — JULY 25.

IT is over a thousand years since St Francis Of Assisi wrote these words, yet I believe they are still the best advice you can give anyone who thinks the task asked is too big, or too difficult to tackle.

The wise St Francis said: "Start by doing what is necessary, then do what is possible; and suddenly you are doing the impossible."

TUESDAY — JULY 26.

THIRTY years or so ago the world was shocked by a picture from the Vietnam War. Kim, a girl who was eight years old, was seen running, in flames, a victim of napalm bombing. She was not expected to survive, yet miraculously she did.

I can't help feeling Kim was spared after her terrible ordeal for a purpose. Now a Christian, she travels the world, spreading the Word, preaching peace.

WEDNESDAY — JULY 27.

THE folk who look happiest,
And those who seem bright,
With smiles on their faces
And feet that are light,
Are not always those
Who have lived in the sun,
But those who faced darkness
And fought it, and won.

THURSDAY — JULY 28.

THERE are many stories about the famous singing group, the Beatles. I once read a moving story about John Lennon who died so tragically, while still relatively young.

I found these words, spoken by his son Sean some time later, touching: "It's not John Lennon, the Beatle, I miss — it's the guy who put me on his shoulder when we walked on the beach together. I miss my dad."

Love is worth far more than fame and riches.

FRIDAY — JULY 29.

I ONCE had a friendly chat with a talented piano player. You had only to mention a melody, and Renee would play it to perfection. But she also added her own interpretation of the music, and sometimes would sing along to it as well.

However, what I recall most clearly is a passing remark she once made before we said our good-byes. She smilingly brushed off our compliments with these words:

"It's the way you look at things. Life is like a piano — what you get out of it depends on how you play it."

Those words are still sweet music to my ears.

SATURDAY — JULY 30.

THERE is an old adage: "When you're a teacher, by your pupils you'll be taught."

I read a more recent story by Gervase Phinn, a Yorkshire schools inspector and author, who tells of an interesting conversation with an eleven-year-old boy in the Dales, a keen reader who solemnly said, "Hold a book in your hand, and you're a pilgrim at the gates of a new city."

A surprising thing for a young lad to say but he had, in fact, learned this Hebrew proverb from his grandfather, a preacher.

SUNDAY — JULY 31.

HEAL me, O Lord, and I shall be healed; save me, and I shall be saved: for thou art my praise.

Jeremiah 17:14

August

OUR friend Joanne was all smiles when she returned from town and told how she read this advice on a poster in a beauty salon:

"Show your best face to the mirror, and you'll be happy with the face looking back at you."

I'm sure the composer of the notice could well have added: ". . . and the world will be happy, too".

NEXT TIME

IT'S easy to miss chances,
When busy on life's way,
Of doing folk a favour,
Or kindness when we may.
Yet when the moment's vanished,
Too late to say, "Oh, dear,"
And wish we'd made the gesture
That might have brought some cheer.
So do not dwell on failings,
Regret them as we might,
Instead, let's make a promise —
Next time we'll get it right!

Margaret Ingall.

ROCKS OF
AGES

WEDNESDAY — AUGUST 3.

YOU wouldn't think you could learn much from a clown, would you? Well, our friend Alan did.

You see, he had suffered a series of hard knocks: his business had folded, he was injured in a car accident, and he was on the point of giving up.

Then he took a friend's children to the circus. "I saw this clown falling down time after time, then getting up again laughing as much as ever, and I thought, I can be like that!" he said.

Alan has fought back and built up another business. Next year he is to be married. And, he says, it's all thanks to a clown!

THURSDAY — AUGUST 4.

WHEN the Lady of the House and I visit our old friend Mary, we always enjoy a delicious lunch. Her one fault — if it can be called that — is that she tends to give us helpings that are sometimes rather too generous.

On one visit not long ago, Mary popped into her kitchen to make coffee, and we noticed these lines framed on the wall:

The more you give,
The more you get.
The more you do unselfishly
The more you live abundantly.
The more of everything you share,
The more you laugh, the less you fret.
The more you love, the more you'll find,
That life is good and friends are kind.

Words we can all ponder on today.

FRIDAY — AUGUST 5.

A LICE was on holiday at the seaside, and one day found herself admiring the shell collection of a little boy sitting on the beach.

"You know," she told me, "until then I had never realised just how many wonderful and subtle variations there can be even in a small sample of cockle shells. Within moments of examining them, I was as engrossed as he was. But I suppose we're usually so busy looking out for the more impressive sights of the world that we forget to pay attention to the smaller marvels."

Sometimes it takes a child to remind us that even the most ordinary objects can be magical if observed through eyes of wonder.

SATURDAY — AUGUST 6.

W HAT a lovely idea to give a town the name Friendship! Our friends, Peter and Sally, went on a motoring holiday in the United States and were pleasantly surprised, while driving through Arkansas, to come suddenly on this sign: "Welcome To Friendship."

Returning home, they checked at their local library, and were surprised to learn there are seven other towns called Friendship in the United States. You'll find a Friendship in Indiana, Maine, Maryland, Wisconsin, Ohio, Tennessee and in New York State.

All small and friendly American towns where the residents are happy to live up to their name, especially on the first Sunday of August, Friendship Day.

SUNDAY — AUGUST 7.

HAVE not I commanded thee? Be strong and of good courage; be not afraid, neither be thou dismayed: for the Lord thy God is with thee whithersoever thou goest. Joshua I:9

MONDAY — AUGUST 8.

ACTORS often, I've noticed, have a positive attitude to changes which the passing years bring.

Stars in their late fifties and sixties are often highly competent character actors. How wrong, then, to think of showbusiness as a world peopled only by glamorous young women and handsome young men!

Lauren Bacall, the widow of Humphrey Bogart, and herself a popular actress for many years, emphatically told an interviewer:

"You've got it wrong, my lad. I'm not a has-been. I am a will-be!"

An opportunity to show our talents can come at any time of our lives.

TUESDAY — AUGUST 9.

I AM not in favour of rigidly categorising people but Alan Cohen, a writer who lives on the Hawaiian island of Maui, has made this interesting comparison.

"There are," he says, "two kinds of people in the world — those who make excuses and those who get results. An excuse person will find any excuse for why a job was not done, and a results person will find any reason why it can be done."

WEDNESDAY — AUGUST 10.

I CAME on these Rules For Happiness, displayed on a church notice-board:
Stop blaming other people.
Be humble.
Listen more; talk less.
Every day, do something nice.
Strive for excellence, not perfection.
Be on time.
Admit it when you make a mistake.
Let someone cut ahead of you in line.
Know when to keep your mouth shut.

THURSDAY — AUGUST 11.

WHILE visiting young Charlie's mother, the Lady of the House and I had fun watching him build a tower of wooden bricks, until a sudden wobble made the whole structure collapse.

Indignantly Charlie turned towards his baby sister, who was sleeping peacefully in her cot. "That was your fault!" he said.

The sheer outrageousness of the accusation was enough to make everyone laugh, but I couldn't help thinking just how easily it comes to us all to sometimes blame others for our mistakes.

Young children have time to learn, but let us try to set a good example by acknowledging responsibilities and doing our best to acquire wisdom from experience.

If we can manage to do that, then I think we have a much better chance of building towers that won't fall down!

THE FRIENDSHIP BOOK

THE writer Karl Schmidt once wrote: "Every sunset is also a sunrise. It all depends on where you stand."

A friend thought of these words during a recent visit abroad. It was the time of the evening in a Florida hotel, when guests gathered to marvel at the magnificent sunset over the Gulf of Mexico.

At that moment, Peter realised that this very same sun was dawning elsewhere in a different time zone.

Now, aren't the hopes and fortunes of life rather like the movement of the sun? For some they are gently descending in a beautiful twilight; for others they are rising with the prospect of a bright new day.

TRUE friendship should be treasured
In life's deceptive maze.
Its value can be measured
In many different ways.
Though certain cynics doubt it
With each dismissive thought,
Make no mistake about it —
True friendship means a lot.

John M. Robertson.

NOW, therefore, I pray thee, pardon my sin, and turn again with me, that I may worship the Lord.
Samuel I 15:25

THE FRIENDSHIP BOOK

<u>MONDAY — AUGUST 15.</u>

HERE'S an amusing tale from a reader's church magazine:

Up at the head table in the school cafeteria, one of the nuns had placed a big bowl of fresh juicy apples. Beside the bowl, she placed a note which read: *Take only one. Remember, God is watching.*

At the other end of the table was a bowl full of freshly-baked chocolate chip cookies, still warm from the oven. Beside the bowl lay a little scrawled note in a child's handwriting which read: *Take all you want. God's watching the apples.*

<u>TUESDAY — AUGUST 16.</u>

*T*HE *golden gorse climbs up the hill*
  Beside the winding lane,
And valley fields turn now to gold
  With slowly ripening grain.
Wild flowers fill the meadow lands,
  A white and gold display,
As cottage gardens bloom once more
  And take our breath away.

Gold sunbeams sparkle on the sea
  And spread along the sand,
Recalling days when youth and love
  Went dancing hand in hand.
Each stream and river, lake and tarn,
  Provide more dreams to hold,
As land and sea and sky rejoice
  And share the Summer's gold.

Iris Hesselden.

WEDNESDAY — AUGUST 17.

IT keeps you smiling when everything seems against you. It keeps you going when up against a brick wall. It keeps you on your feet when you should be down and out.

What is it? Faith. If you have that, you don't need anything else.

*F*aith
*A*chieves
*I*mpossible
*T*hings
*H*umbly.

THURSDAY — AUGUST 18.

A YOUNG friend had just handed in some of her clothes to a charity shop. "They had gone out of fashion," she explained.

I was reminded of two quotations. First Shakespeare's: "Fashion wears out more apparel than the man."

The other is from Ambrose Bierce who said that fashion is "a despot whom the wise ridicule — and obey!"

You will not be surprised to hear that I mentioned neither of these, nor the well-known saying, "Fashion makes fools of us all!"

FRIDAY — AUGUST 19.

TIME for a little smile, courtesy of the ubiquitous "Anon".

"Where there is smoke, there's toast."

"Punctuality is something that, if you have it, there's often no one around to share it with you."

SATURDAY — AUGUST 20.

IT'S a sad irony that sometimes, when our hearts are at their most full, we find it hardest to tell God how we are feeling. I was pleased to come across the following quotation which seems to say it all:

"God understands our prayers even when we can't find the words to say them."

It's not known who first wrote these words, but it's certainly a comforting thought to remember when the problems of the world seem too big for us to cope with.

SUNDAY — AUGUST 21.

BUT unto the Son he saith, Thy throne, O God, is for ever and ever: a sceptre of righteousness is the sceptre of thy kingdom.

Hebrews 1:8

MONDAY — AUGUST 22.

AGATHA CHRISTIE, the famous mystery writer, wove many a human story into the tapestry of her novels and she enjoyed a long and successful career until her death in 1976.

Not everyone realises, however, that behind the public image of many well-known figures, there exists all the usual doubts and frailties which can affect the rest of us. This came to mind when I found this thought one day from Agatha Christie's writings:

"I like living. I have sometimes been wildly, despairingly, acutely miserable, racked with sorrow, but through it all I still know quite certainly that just to be alive is a grand thing."

TUESDAY — AUGUST 23.

A YOUNG friend of ours has reached the point in his school life when he has to start dropping some subjects, and concentrate on a few.

"Chemistry or physics?" he asked his parents. "History or modern studies?"

It's not easy to make that kind of decision when you don't know what the future holds. Everyone has advice to give, but most of us will admit that we have made a few wrong choices in our lives.

However, sometimes a decision just has to be made, and although it can turn out to be the wrong one, it's worthwhile learning from the past. As Soren Kierkegaard said, "Life can only be understood backwards, but it still has to be lived forwards."

WEDNESDAY — AUGUST 24.

O UR friend Harriet saw these words on a poster. Think about them today —

Nothing wastes more energy than worrying. The longer a problem is carried, the heavier it gets.

THURSDAY — AUGUST 25.

Y OU might not think our friend Dora had much to be thankful for. Life had given her many unexpected setbacks. Yet she started every new day counting up all the things she felt grateful for.

"And I don't know how it is," she said with a smile, "but the list grows longer every morning!"

The secret is this: count your blessings and they multiply, ignore them and they fade away.

FRIDAY — AUGUST 26.

SUMMER STORM

BLACK clouds across the brooding
mountain spill,
And cast their sombre shadows on the plain.
A gusty wind comes sweeping down the hill,
Pursuing veils of rain.

Then sunlight gilds the summit of the ben,
The last torn rags of cloud are blown away,
And, shimmering above the patchwork glen,
A rainbow promises a perfect day.

Brenda G. Macrow.

SATURDAY — AUGUST 27.

IT is a good idea for us to enjoy a hobby which takes us into a world contrasting with that of our everyday life. George Bruce, a well-known broadcaster, was 93 when he died in Edinburgh after a lifetime devoted to the arts.

Obituaries told of his long life as a poet and a man of letters but when I read them, the item that impressed me most was the choice of his main recreation. This, he said, was "visiting friends".

I think you'll agree that he couldn't have chosen better.

SUNDAY — AUGUST 28.

AND the people said unto Joshua, The Lord our God will we serve, and his voice will we obey.

Joshua 24:24

AS GOOD AS IT GETS

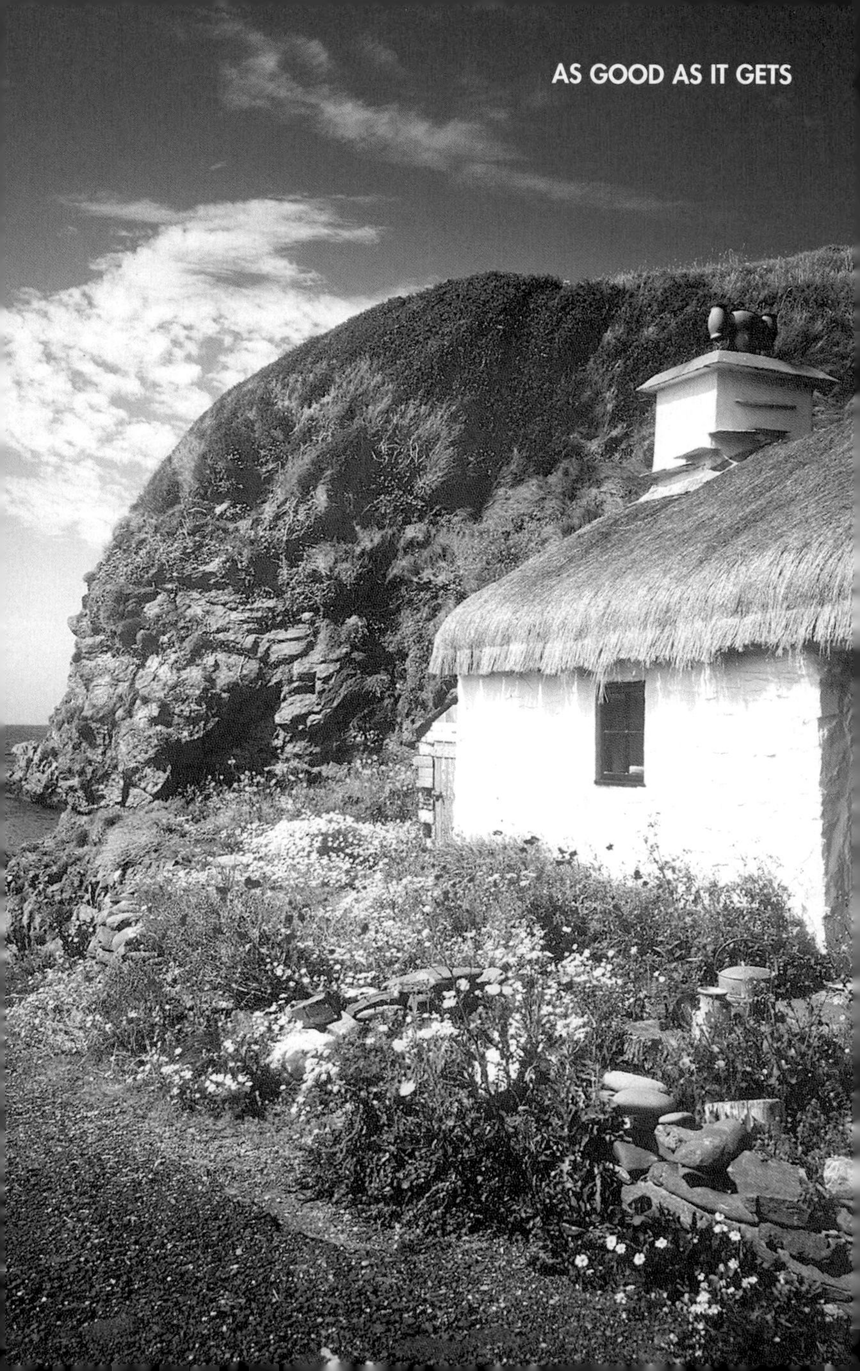

MONDAY — AUGUST 29.

ROSEMARY Verey caught the gardening bug in the 1950s. She wrote many books and created a garden at her home in Gloucestershire which delighted thousands of visitors.

To a ripe age she rose every morning at six o'clock and, as she began work, she would say aloud, "Today something exciting is going to happen."

What a lovely way to start any morning!

TUESDAY — AUGUST 30.

I WAS joining one day in that often-heard conversation about the cost of living when the Lady of the House interrupted me and, with a knowing smile, said:

"Yes, we all know, Francis, that living on earth is expensive but, remember, it does include a free trip around the sun every year."

I had to admit that, as the song says, we've got the moon at night as well. Nature compensates us, indeed!

WEDNESDAY — AUGUST 31.

HERE are two thoughts to remember on one of those rather drab days when you may be struggling to remain in good spirits:

"The art of being happy lies in the power of extracting happiness from common things."

"Life does not require us to be the biggest or the best. It only asks that we try."

I think you'll agree that there's a lot of sound sense here.

September

THURSDAY — SEPTEMBER 1.

IT is good to inspire our friends and neighbours. I call it the art of encouraging others.

Here from our old friend Anon is a useful piece of advice: "You get the best effort from others not by lighting a fire beneath them, but by building a fire within."

A wise thought to take to heart, I think you will agree.

FRIDAY — SEPTEMBER 2.

MY FAVOURITE MONTH

SEPTEMBER, September, I love you so
  Your golden light, your russet glow,
Of all the months none can compare
  With harvest fruits of plum and pear.

Of mellow days of sweet content
  Of ripened berry heaven sent,
Of woodland walks of tawny brown
  Where leaves of copper filter down.

And spider with his jewel-like web
  And robin with his breast of red,
A time that surely God has blessed
  September is, for me, the best.

Eva Knights.

SATURDAY — SEPTEMBER 3.

ONE Sunday morning the weather was dreadful. It was cold, wet and a strong wind was beating against the church windows. The visiting clergyman that day surveyed the subdued congregation in front of him.

He commenced by saying, "You know, I like to start services with these words: 'Let us thank God this morning for . . .' then add whatever blessing is appropriate at that time.

"However, on a morning like this I have to say, 'Let us thank the Lord every morning is not as bad as this!'"

Everyone laughed and a cheerful, enjoyable service followed. There is always something to thank God for if we just take a few moments to think about it.

SUNDAY — SEPTEMBER 4.

BELOVED, if God so loved us, we ought also to love one another.

John I 4:11

MONDAY — SEPTEMBER 5.

HAVE you ever been on the receiving end of the best kind of smile, when the eyes of the person smiling at you light up and twinkle?

A generous, kind, warm smile, meant just for you. A cheerful smile which says, "Isn't it grand to be alive?" It is a delightful sort of smile; you will find yourself spontaneously smiling back.

Now, how do your own smiles rate? Are they the best kind or is there room for improvement?

THE FRIENDSHIP BOOK

TUESDAY — SEPTEMBER 6.

IT'S at this time of year that Sylvia always starts thinking about which adult education courses to enrol in. She takes much care in choosing which class to attend, and usually decides upon something creative, such as weaving, painting or pottery.

I once asked her what she enjoyed making most of all.

"I'll give you three guesses," she said. "It's something I've made in almost every class I've ever attended, and which I always hope will last a lifetime."

I must have looked baffled, for she laughed. "It's easy, Francis," she explained. "The answer is friends!"

Now what could be more enjoyable to make than that?

WEDNESDAY — SEPTEMBER 7.

THERE'S a saying: "A hug is a very special gift; it can always be returned and one size fits all." There's a rhyme, too, which goes:

It's funny how a little hug
Makes everyone feel good —
In every place and language,
It's always understood.
Hugs don't need new equipment,
Special batteries, or parts —
Just open up your arms
And open up your hearts!

The precious moments of living get a new significance when we add hugs to them.

THURSDAY — SEPTEMBER 8.

A FRIEND, Flora, received a letter from a young relative who felt that life was not treating her too kindly. Flora sent back this reply:

God didn't promise days without pain,
Laughter without sorrow,
Sun without rain,
But He did promise you
Strength for the day,
Comfort for the tears,
And light for the way!

Then she added this PS: "Remember this — He sends you flowers every Spring, and light every morning."

FRIDAY — SEPTEMBER 9.

WHEN Dolly and Arthur moved into their new house many years ago they inherited a fine row of apple trees in the back garden.

"For years, the apple tree on the left-hand side bore no fruit at all," Dolly said. "Then it suddenly started producing little red apples. The next year, not so many — but the cookers had a ball." Dolly made apple crumble, apple turnovers and her special spicy apple chutney which filled a multitude of attractively-decorated jars.

"You know, Francis," the Lady of the House mused later, "I reckon it's the same with some of us. We have times when nothing much happens. Then — all at once — it's abundance. And that's when we have to get our sleeves rolled up and make our apple crumble, turnovers and spicy apple chutney!"

SATURDAY — SEPTEMBER 10.

D ESPITE all the wonders of modern science, the basic recipe for our daily bread remains the same, as this old rhyme tells:

Back of the loaf is the snowy flour,
And back of the flour is the mill,
And back of the mill is the wheat and the shower,
And the sun and the Father's will.

SUNDAY — SEPTEMBER 11.

A ND after these things I heard a great voice of much people in heaven, saying, Alleluia; Salvation, and glory, and honour, and power, unto the Lord our God.   Revelation 19:1

MONDAY — SEPTEMBER 12.

A S a child, Ruth lacked confidence. She doubted her own worth and abilities, until one year her aunt gave her a diary. "Try to write down something you've achieved every day," she urged. "However small it seems."

Ruth promised to do her best, and at the end of the year was duly asked what she'd recorded. Glowing, the girl showed her aunt the diary. It was full of entries, ranging from such simple things such as "Helped Mother with her patchwork", to "Won first prize for my essay".

The change in Ruth was remarkable, not because she had more achievements to her credit but simply because she had bothered to take note of them. So, next time you feel inadequate, pay more attention to your accomplishments — and to those of others!

THE FRIENDSHIP BOOK

I F hope takes a tumble
And all your dreams crumble,
Hold fast to things you believe.
And, never despairing,
Undaunted and daring
Remember, you still can achieve.

Though others alarm you,
Dismay or disarm you
And think your ambitions have fled,
The future is changing,
Your life rearranging,
The road to success lies ahead!

Iris Hesselden.

I LIKE this story straight from the kitchen which shows how, when life gets tough, the key to success lies in how we respond.

Take three pots and turn up the heat until the water in each is boiling. Put carrots in the first pot, an egg in the second, and coffee grounds in the third.

Turn off the heat, and we find the carrots have softened, the egg is hardened, and the grounds have created a pot of rich-flavoured coffee.

Each item has faced an adverse situation, but each has responded differently to the boiling heat.

Let's never think of adversity as an enemy. It gives us an opportunity to change the situation and conditions around us, and make us all the stronger.

THURSDAY — SEPTEMBER 15.

HAVE you ever resolved upon offering someone a kindly word, doing a good deed or simply standing up for something you believe in — but then not actually got round to doing it?

It happens easily, I know. We start off with the intention of trying our best to make the world a better place, but often it never quite happens.

Next time we're tempted to put off acting upon a higher impulse, it's worth remembering the words of John Ruskin, who wrote: "What we think, or what we know, or what we believe is, in the end, of little consequence. The only consequence is what we do."

So next time let's determine that we will do it, instead of just planning to!

FRIDAY — SEPTEMBER 16.

I WAS once told about a farmer in the American Mid-West who entered his corn in the annual State Fair and always won a prize. It emerged that he was sharing his seed corn with his neighbours.

"How can you afford to share your best seed corn when others are entering corn in competition with yours?" he was asked.

"Well," said the farmer, "the wind picks up pollen from my ripening corn and swirls it from field to field. If my neighbours grow inferior corn, cross-pollination will steadily ruin the quality of my corn, so if I am to grow good corn, I must help my neighbours."

To live well, we must help others to live well. To stay happy, we must help others find happiness.

SATURDAY — SEPTEMBER 17.

ROBERT was in full flow one evening as he explained why he believes in adopting a positive attitude to life.

"Each morning I wake up and say to myself, 'Robert, you have two choices today. You can choose to be in a good mood or you can choose to be in a bad mood.' I choose to be in a good mood.

"Then, each time something untoward happens, I can choose to be a victim or I can choose to learn from it. I choose to learn from it.

"Every time someone comes to me complaining, I can choose to accept their complaining or I can point out the positive side to life. I choose the positive side."

As Robert says, "Life is all about choices."

SUNDAY — SEPTEMBER 18.

WHEN a man's ways please the Lord, he maketh even his enemies to be at peace with him.
                                                    Proverbs 16:7

MONDAY — SEPTEMBER 19.

I IMAGINE most of us have heard of Will Rogers, the part-Cherokee American whose career ranged from humble cowboy to movie star.

He was also a philanthropist who used his money to help many charitable causes, and a philosopher who was never dazzled by his own fame. "It's great to be great," he once said, "but it's greater to be human."

Now *that* kind of attitude is something we can all aspire to.

TUESDAY — SEPTEMBER 20.

MOLLY lives in a village in the country. It's a pretty little place, but when she first moved in, it bothered her that no-one seemed interested in keeping it looking nice. She fretted that "they" never picked up litter, or kept the green looking tidy.

"Then one day," she said, "it occurred to me that any kind of improvement has to start somewhere, so the 'somewhere' might just as well be me. The next time I went out, I took a bag and collected litter as I went. Soon people were complimenting me on my good work, and before I knew it, we had a regular team on duty.

"But it didn't stop there. Once the roads and verges began to look good, I noticed that people were smartening up their gardens, putting out hanging baskets — even giving their houses a lick of paint! Now, with the whole community pulling together, our village is a joy to see."

What a good reminder that the road to improvement can begin at our own front door.

WEDNESDAY — SEPTEMBER 21.

*E*VERY *chapter in life's journey*
  Plays its own important part,
And by trusting in God's wisdom,
  Hope stays strong within the heart.
There's a purpose in His planning,
  Guiding us within his way,
And our faith, will surely lead us
  To the promise of each day . . .

Elizabeth Gozney.

STILL MILL

THURSDAY — SEPTEMBER 22.

SIR Edmund Hillary and his Sherpa guide Tenzing were the first men to climb Mount Everest but, when they were coming back down from the peak, Hillary suddenly lost his footing.

It was a tense moment; at the risk of his own life, Tenzing held the line tight and kept them both from falling off the mountain.

Later, Tenzing simply said, "Mountain climbers always help each other."

We are all climbing up and down the mountains of life, so let's make sure we are on hand to help when someone slips off course.

FRIDAY — SEPTEMBER 23.

WHEN Neil agreed to play a piece on the piano at the annual church get-together, he felt rather nervous. He had never played in public before and had been having lessons for only a few months.

People were surprised when he walked to the piano and announced, "Ladies and gentlemen, I would like to play for you Rachmaninoff's Prelude in C Sharp Minor." He paused, then said with a grin, "Unfortunately, I don't know how to. It's much too difficult for me, but isn't it marvellous that there are people who can play to such a high standard. But as I'm not one of them, I will play something else for you instead . . ."

He played a simple, yet melodious beginners' piece and received appreciative applause. We can enrich our lives by enjoying the talent of others, great or small.

THE FRIENDSHIP BOOK

I'VE been hearing about the work of Hannah More. Born near Bristol in 1745, it was obvious, even as a child, that she was a natural scholar. Once grown up, she soon became a successful writer, but was equally keen to use her gifts to help others, which is why her name has lived on as a philanthropist, evangelist and pioneer of Sunday schools.

With such a record, it is perhaps not so remarkable that Hannah was once quoted as observing that, "Obstacles are those frightful things you see when you take your eyes off the goal."

A remark to remember when our own goals seem impossibly hard to reach.

FOR he looked for a city which hath foundations, whose builder and maker is God.

Hebrews 11:10

HERE are some wise words to think about if you are about to join the commuter rush into work today and find yourself going at a faster-than-you-need speed just to keep up with your fellow-travellers:

"Don't run through life so fast that you forget not only where you've been, but also where you are going. Life is not a race, but a beautiful and pleasant journey to be savoured each step of the way."

THE FRIENDSHIP BOOK

TUESDAY — SEPTEMBER 27.

ELIZABETH left school early. She was very talented artistically — in fact, so good that her art teacher said she should stay on at school, then go to art college. But although Elizabeth wanted to do so, she was one of a large family, where unemployment was a familiar shadow, and so she had to earn a wage immediately after leaving school.

At first, Elizabeth worked in a factory, and then later she married a much-loved man, and they had a son and daughter. There was still very little money, so Elizabeth continued to work as she'd always done. People talk about the ache of an unused talent; it was something she knew all about. Suddenly, though, retirement brought time to attend art classes, with weeks on end to draw and paint to her heart's content.

There is a saying that opportunity knocks only once. Well, perhaps sometimes, but not always, for it knocked twice for Elizabeth. So do remember to answer the door, if a knock sounds for you!

WEDNESDAY — SEPTEMBER 28.

RON has a youthful outlook on life. On his birthday last year he put on his most innocent-looking expression, and told his many friends:

"You know, I'm not sixty. I'm eighteen with forty-two years' experience."

Isn't that as positive a way as any of looking at a milestone birthday?

THURSDAY — SEPTEMBER 29.

OUR friend Karen dislikes people who gossip. She often reminds friends: "Speak sweetly, so that, if you have to eat your words, they won't taste so bad."

Truly good advice to give, I'd say. Like that other gem handed down by a wise lady ninety years young:

"Always remember that you are the proud owner of a set of ears; use them at your own discretion."

FRIDAY — SEPTEMBER 30.

GARDENER'S REWARD

LIFE is like a garden
And if we look around,
Many fine examples
Of comparisons are found.

Plant the seed of kindness,
And it is bound to grow
If fertilised by friendship
To bring a special glow.

Call a spade a spade and learn
To dig out misery.
Transplant toleration
Where confusion used to be.

Life is like a garden
Of that, there's little doubt,
And even more so when the threat
Of worry's weeded out.

J. M. Robertson.

October

OUTSIDE a church gate I picked up a discarded piece of paper. Thinking it could be a church notice of some kind, I opened and read it.

At the top, in neat writing, was the date and the heading "Things To Be Grateful For Today". It was a list of ten items, including: "Finding That Secondhand Bookshop, Buying That Old Book, Seeing Those Puppies, Catching The Bus On Time and Meeting A Friend Again".

Simple things, perhaps, but all obviously important to the writer. I was about to throw it into the nearby bin when, on impulse, I tucked it under the windscreen wipers of the clergyman's car, parked nearby.

Food for thought or maybe even an idea for the next sermon? That unknown person had the right idea. Perhaps we should all make a list every day and, in time, "Things To Be Grateful For" would far outnumber "Things To Grumble About"!

THINE eyes shall see the king in his beauty: they shall behold the land that is very far off.

Isaiah 33:17

THE FRIENDSHIP BOOK

MONDAY — OCTOBER 3.

IT was a day to lift the heart. A still October day of gentle blue skies and soft, misty sunshine, a golden day, which reminded me of those beautiful lines by the poet Shelley:

The day becomes more solemn and serene,
When noon is past — there is a harmony
In Autumn, and a lustre in its sky,
Which through the Summer is not heard or seen.

TUESDAY — OCTOBER 4.

TODAY I feel like becoming a "possibilitarian". This word was invented by Norman Vincent Peale, who rose from poverty to become a best-selling writer. It refers to a person who, no matter how dark things are, raises his sights.

Norman, born in 1898 in Findlay, Ohio, helped to support his family by delivering newspapers, working in a grocery store and selling pots and pans from door to door. He became a reporter on his local newspaper and then moved on to inspire millions as one of the most influential preachers in the USA.

His books of uplifting words and sermons sold millions of copies worldwide. There is, Norman told his friends, "a real magic in enthusiasm". Among his tips for living he listed: "Get interested in something. Get enthralled. The more you lose yourself in something bigger than yourself, the more energy you will have."

He died in 1993, leaving this message: "People lose energy only when life becomes dull in their mind. It's the doing nothing that makes them tired and bored."

WEDNESDAY — OCTOBER 5.

FRIENDS of ours have a sixteen-year-old cat, Phoebe, who has been with them since she was a kitten.

"One of the hardest things to do now she's getting older," Lynn told me, "is to put her out at night, especially when it's wet and windy. However, she has shelter in the garden shed, and it's something we've always done. It's part of her routine.

"And we've noticed that in the mornings her fur is fresher and in better condition after a shower of rain. It's almost as if that little bit of hardship is good for her."

It struck me that it's often that way in life. We can be tried and tested, yet often we emerge from hardship all the stronger for it.

As the apostle Paul wrote in his letter to the Romans: ". . . suffering produces perseverance; perseverance character and character hope".

THURSDAY — OCTOBER 6.

I DON'T know who he was but one windy Autumn day I met an elderly gentleman walking in a beech wood.

"Sad to see the leaves falling," I said in passing.

He shook his head and smiled. "In time they will turn to mould to feed these trees and others that come after them."

I was grateful to be reminded that the dropping leaves are not the end of something but part of a continual process of renewal. It makes a difference when you look at it that way, doesn't it?

FRIDAY — OCTOBER 7.

A NINETEEN-YEAR-OLD girl once asked a woman aged ninety-two to give her a tip for happy living. Here's what she was told:

"Be kind each day to all the people you meet, for every second person may well be having a harder time than you."

I wonder how many uncertain moments have been turned around and how many days made the brighter by a friend or stranger offering a small word of kindness. We can easily forget that tears of sadness are frequently kept hidden in the eyes of the people we meet.

SATURDAY — OCTOBER 8.

I N the staff canteen of a big city office I once came on this notice which was pinned to the wall:—

LITTLE THINGS

Do little things to brighten up
The spot on which you're standing
By being more considerate
And a pickle less demanding.

Our dark old world would very soon
Eclipse the evening star,
If each of us would brighten up
The corner where we are.

SUNDAY — OCTOBER 9.

W HILE I live will I praise the Lord: I will sing praises unto my God while I have any being.

Psalms 146:2

THE FRIENDSHIP BOOK

WHEN a careless servant burned the manuscript of Thomas Carlyle's great work "The French Revolution", a lesser man might have given up. Many months of hard work had been destroyed.

It was a terrible blow but, said Carlyle later, "It came to me that, as they lay brick on brick, so I could still lay word on word, sentence on sentence."

That was what he did, patiently re-writing page after page until it was finished. It was, he said, all the better for being written twice!

LIFE'S CROSSROADS

THIS life is a series of crossroads,
The meeting and parting of ways,
The places we look for a signpost
To guide us through life's tangled maze.
The path may be sunlit and cheerful,
Wild flowers bloom bright in the hedge,
The distant horizon be hopeful
And offer a promise and pledge.

But then as the crossroads draw nearer,
Dark shadows obscure all the view,
And which way to turn is the problem,
The words on the signpost are few.
Each time you arrive at a junction
And you have decisions to make,
Be true to yourself and have courage,
And you'll know which pathway to take!
Iris Hesselden.

THE FRIENDSHIP BOOK

<u>WEDNESDAY — OCTOBER 12.</u>

MORAG, who is a romantic kind of person, was telling us one day how she likes to see a young couple clasping hands, looking into each other's eyes, showing the world they are in love.

"Is there anything more beautiful in life than young love?" she asked.

Nell could hardly wait to speak.

"Yes, there is something every bit as beautiful as young love," she chimed in. "It's when you see an elderly couple walking along the street together. Their hands are gnarled but still clasped; their faces are lined but still radiant; their hearts may be physically tired, but they are still stronger than ever with love and devotion for one another.

"That, to me, is as beautiful as young love, and I've a name for it. I call it 'Lasting Love'."

A perfect description.

<u>THURSDAY — OCTOBER 13.</u>

WHAT would I do without my friend,
No matter where life's roads I wend,
He is always by my side,
To help me if I slip or slide,
We've been together now for years,
Thro' times of happiness and tears,
On the hilltops capped with snow,
Or in green valleys down below,
In Winter, Summer, Autumn, Spring,
Self assurance he will bring,
My friend, my pal, my old sidekick —
My well-worn, wooden walking stick!

Brian H. Gent.

THE FRIENDSHIP BOOK

"YOU know," observed the Lady of the House putting down a newspaper one morning, "I'm sure there are some people in this world who are never happy unless they are miserable."

I had to agree, for I certainly know one or two like that — the person who expects bad news by every post and those who take gloomy pleasure in forecasting all kinds of misfortune, from bad weather to world disaster.

Now I know it's not possible, or even desirable, to go through life relying on blind optimism, but I'm still a great believer in the power of positive thinking to help smooth the way. As Mark Twain once humorously remarked, "Nobody knows the troubles I've seen, and most of them never happened."

So do make sure that you don't see troubles that don't exist!

WHAT are the hardest words to say in the English language? My friend Duncan has no doubts. Not long married, he and his wife had a row and he said things he at once regretted. Next morning he spoke the difficult words: "I'm sorry."

They sound easy but because people find them so hard to say, marriages break down and friendships are lost.

However, I'm glad that Duncan learned to say them and that, in return, he heard some of the sweetest words in the English language: "I forgive you."

THE FRIENDSHIP BOOK

SUNDAY — OCTOBER 16.

TAKE my yoke upon you, and learn of me; for I am meek and lowly in heart: and ye shall find rest unto your souls. Matthew 11:29

MONDAY — OCTOBER 17.

THE all-embracing world of the Internet allows us to communicate across the world at the click of a computer mouse. Millions enjoy sending letters and family photographs by e-mail; many new contacts are made, and long-standing ones cherished.

Hilda, a friend of ours, made a good point one afternoon when we were discussing the business of making and keeping friends.

"Remember, Francis," she said. "We can easily get into the habit of chatting several times a day online with folk in Australia or South Africa, and forget that we haven't spoken to our next-door neighbour for a week."

A gentle word of warning for us all to heed.

TUESDAY — OCTOBER 18.

GEMS OF FRIENDSHIP

SOMEONE to listen,
Someone to care,
Someone whose presence
  By just being there
Can bring us the comfort
  To soothe us in need,
True gems of friendship
  To treasure, indeed!
  Elizabeth Gozney.

WEDNESDAY — OCTOBER 19.

THE weather, when it is bad, can get us all down. It is, after all, only natural to feel sad when the clouds are dark and there is heavy rain.

William Arthur Ward wrote: "A cloudy day is no match for a sunny disposition." How true — meet a cheerful friend or associate, and their positive outlook helps to brighten the day.

I sometimes quote this extract from the works of author A. A. Milne, who was a journalist on the magazine "Punch" before he became famous as an author of children's books, including "Winnie The Pooh".

"Hello, Eeyore," said Christopher Robin, as he opened the door and came out. "How are you?"

"It's snowing still," said Eeyore, gloomily.

"So it is."

"And freezing."

"Is it?"

"Yes," said Eeyore. "However," he said, brightening up a little, "we haven't had an earthquake lately."

THURSDAY — OCTOBER 20.

GEORGE is one of the keenest gardeners in his village. I met him one day standing at his garden gate.

"Busy day as usual, George?" I enquired.

"I've just been planting a hundred bulbs to greet me in Spring," he replied. "You know, Francis, I always call that 'Making a contract with the future'. I can count on Nature honouring the contract with a fine splash of colour."

FRIDAY — OCTOBER 21.

TOM was staring up at the silver dot of an aeroplane high above in the blue sky when I arrived.

"I was reading last night," he told me, "of just how many early aviation pioneers died in the attempt to achieve flight. And now planes go everywhere, reuniting friends and families, and giving all sorts of ordinary folk the chance to meet new people and visit faraway places."

Standing beside him, I, too, gazed up into the sky. So often those who chase their dreams are regarded as fools, yet without them how many benefits would have remained lost to society?

So three cheers for those visionaries; without them the world would undoubtedly be a poorer place.

SATURDAY — OCTOBER 22.

BEAUTIFUL WORLD

THIS world's so full of beauty,
Don't pass it by each day
Ignoring all the wonders
Beside you on your way.
The dancing days of Springtime,
The Summer's comely face,
The burnished gold of Autumn,
The Winter's silver grace,
These all are gifts of glory
Bestowed with loving care,
So stop and see the beauty
That's here for all to share.

Margaret Ingall.

WALK THIS
WAY

SUNDAY — OCTOBER 23.

AND the gospel must first be published among all nations.

Mark 13:10

MONDAY — OCTOBER 24.

YOU can't beat old ideas. Sydney Smith, writer and clergyman, inspired the society of his day by proposing: "Let us try, each day, to make at least one person happy.

"This way," he said, "each one of us, in ten years, will have made three thousand, six hundred and fifty people happy.

"By the same estimate we will have brightened an entire small town through our contribution to a remarkable fund, the fund of general enjoyment."

Smith, who lived from 1771 to 1845, planned to add brightness to a world not always eager to smile and be happy. Now, wouldn't it be an idea to start repeating his idea today?

TUESDAY — OCTOBER 25.

ONE late October day, our old friend Mary said, "The dark days of Winter are about to arrive. I feel so down when Autumn slips away."

But I reminded her of these wise words:

"In a way Winter is the real Spring, the time when the inner things happen, the resurge of nature."

Edna O'Brien.

"Let us love Winter, for it is the Spring of genius."

Pietro Aretino.

THE FRIENDSHIP BOOK

MIRIAM was telling me she is a member of a multi-cultural club. "Yes, we have great fun," she laughed. "We have so many different beliefs and customs. I think of us as like a lot of crayons, all sorts of colours but all learning to live together in the same box."

Come to think of it, that's a good description of the peoples of the world, isn't it?

WHEN asked what had been the most important thing he had learned at school, Simon surprised his friends by saying that it was not any particular subject. It was, in fact, a line from the school song: "He who rules must first obey."

Those words, he said, had helped him so much at the start of his career, and even now, they reminded him that he was never too old to learn something new.

I think this is wise advice for us all.

SUSAN Coolidge, born in Cleveland, Ohio, in 1835, wrote these encouraging lines:

Every day is a fresh beginning;
Listen my soul to the glad refrain.
In spite of old sorrows
And older sinning,
Troubles forecasted
And possible pain,
Take heart with the day and begin again.

SATURDAY — OCTOBER 29.

I ONCE met a man who said his life was so busy he could never find the time to do all the things he wanted to do. I sympathised, then suggested that he might take action by altering his over-crowded lifestyle.

This problem faces us all — just how do we manage our time between work and leisure? Ralph Waldo Emerson, the famous thinker, wrote:

"The present time, like all times, is a very good one, if we but knew what to do with it."

Brian Tracy is an American who offers good ideas to business associates working hard to make better use of their time.

"What counts in the end," he tells them, "is the quantity of the time you spend at home and the quality of the time you give to your work. We should never mix those two things up."

SUNDAY — OCTOBER 30.

THE Lord seeth not as man seeth: for man looketh on the outward appearance, but the Lord looketh on the heart. — Samuel 1 16:7

MONDAY — OCTOBER 31.

WE all go through spells of rough weather and it is sometimes easy to feel helpless when tossed about on life's seas.

Next time you are buffeted by adversity, just remember this: we can't change the direction of the wind, but we can adjust our sails and steer a different course.

November

OUR old friend Mary, who has laughingly referred to herself as "one of the dreamers of the world", has taken to heart the motto: "One day at a time".

It is the title of a popular song that encourages us not to try to do too much at once. Among many others, authors toiling over manuscripts have been given inspiration by this adage.

The Great American Novel, for instance, is credited as being written one page at a time, and the same surely applies to any task demanding continuous effort and application.

Go steadily and gradually. It's a good watchword for each and every day.

SURELY one of the saddest things in life is to regret the lost opportunities for friendship and kindness once a friend or close relative has died.

So if there's a small kindness you could do, a promised letter to write or perhaps even a quick word on the phone just to say hello, then why not do it today?

Or even better . . . why not do it right NOW!

THURSDAY — NOVEMBER 3.

WHEN Reg's wife died, he was inconsolable. They had been married for many years and he missed her so much. He stopped going to the bowling club and stayed in a lot, staring glumly at the television. Then, one day, he had a visit from his old friend, Alf.

"Here's some baking from my wife," he said briskly, "and I'm thirsty after the walk here. Why don't you put on the kettle?"

Reg roused himself, suddenly glad of his friend's company and soon they were enjoying tea and home baking, chatting away.

"Now why don't you come down to the bowling club tomorrow night?" asked Alf. "We're all missing you."

He did just that and gradually, he found that being with his old chums and the challenge of a bowling match was just what he needed. A friendly word of encouragement, knowing someone cared, was enough to start him back on a more positive path.

That's what friends are for — to care, share and be there in times of need.

FRIDAY — NOVEMBER 4.

TO look up and not down,
To look forward and not back,
To look out and not in and
To lend a hand.

Surely those are helpful, wise words from the pen of the Victorian writer E. E. Hale to help us achieve a positive outlook on life.

THE FRIENDSHIP BOOK

SATURDAY — NOVEMBER 5.

OUR friend Gillian heard talking and giggling coming from her twin daughters' bedroom long after she had said goodnight. She went upstairs to have a word with them.

"Quiet, girls!" she said. "It's time you were both asleep. Now, just settle down."

"But that's exactly what we were doing," Hannah said, trying to suppress her laughter.

"Oh, no, you weren't!" replied Gillian, getting rather cross. "I could hear you when I was in the sitting-room."

"Well," explained Alison, "we were telling God jokes. You see, we thought He must be tired of hearing sad stories all the time so we were trying to cheer Him up."

Gillian had no answer to that. She kissed her daughters goodnight and said her own silent prayer of thanks.

SUNDAY — NOVEMBER 6.

FOR he that is mighty hath done to me great things; and holy is his name.

Luke 1:49

MONDAY — NOVEMBER 7.

HERE is a fine thought for all those who love to cherish their dreams and keep aiming high:

"Far away there, in the sunshine, are my highest aspirations. I may not reach them, but I can, now and always, look up, see their beauty, believe in them, and make it my constant aim to reach them."

HIGH AND
MIGHTY

THE FRIENDSHIP BOOK

THERE are many ways to spend time, but these should surely come high on our list of priorities:

Take time to pray — it's a source of power.
Take time to read — it's a fountain of
wisdom.
Take time to play — it's a secret of youth.
Take time to be friendly — it's a path of
happiness.
Take time to laugh — it's the music of the soul.
Take time to dream — it's a road to greater
vision.

BENEDICTION

THE sun is slipping down the sky
And sinking out of sight,
I watch the ever-deepening dusk
Fast fading into night.
The trees stand out in silhouette
Against the evening sky,
A lonesome bird speeds on its way
I hear its plaintive cry.

A quiet peace steals over all
This is the hour of rest,
Nothing seems to move or stir
In burrow, hedge or nest.
As the shades of evening fall
And shadows dance and play,
Nature gives a benediction
On the closing day.

Kathleen Gillum.

THURSDAY — NOVEMBER 10.

ANNE and Dave threw an unusual party for their friends one evening — a photograph party! Guests had to bring along a snapshot of themselves from another time in their lives, each enclosed in an envelope. They were dropped into a box, and after a buffet supper the guessing of who was who began.

Now, just who was that beautiful baby with the curls, and that small boy with the gap-toothed smile riding a donkey at the seaside? And was that young couple photographed with the leaning Tower of Pisa in the background really Matthew and his wife Rosemary?

It was an evening which gave rise to many smiles and reminiscences. Matthew and Rosemary recalled how hard they had saved for so long to go on that trip to Italy a short time after they were married, and how very much they had enjoyed it.

At the end of the evening everyone agreed that it had been a splendid way to spend a Winter's evening. There had been good company and precious memories had been shared. Needless to say, plans were made to meet again soon.

Friendship is like a fine wine, it only gets better with age.

FRIDAY — NOVEMBER 11.

IF your mirror tells you that your age is beginning to show, then think of these words from Alistair Cooke:

"Wrinkles are the credentials of humanity."

SATURDAY — NOVEMBER 12.

ONE cold Winter night two elderly people were seeking accommodation in a small hotel, only to be told by the receptionist, "Sorry, all the rooms are full."

As they were about to leave, the receptionist asked, "Would you be willing to sleep in my room?" They were reluctant but then he added that he himself could sleep in the office, and the couple then accepted his offer.

The next morning the man said to the receptionist, "You should be manager of the best hotel in the country — one day I'll build you one." The receptionist simply smiled and thanked him.

However, a few years later he was surprised when the same couple asked him to visit them in New York. He went, was shown round a huge hotel, then was told that it was built for him to manage. The old gentleman had been none other than the famous William Waldorf Astor!

We never know where a deed of kindness may lead.

SUNDAY — NOVEMBER 13.

AND they departed, and went through the towns, preaching the gospel, and healing every where.   Luke 9:6

MONDAY — NOVEMBER 14.

FRENCH proverbs seem to abound in sayings which are memorable and here is an example: "Adversity is the touchstone of friendship."
How true; fair weather friends need not apply.

TUESDAY — NOVEMBER 15.

THE humdrum world keeps turning round
  It waits beyond my door,
But now and then I let it go
  And find escape once more.
I see the skeins across the sky
  I hear them strangely crying,
And I find freedom in my thoughts,
  I join the wild geese flying.

We all have trouble in our lives
  Sometimes it holds us fast,
And many people find release
  By looking to the past.
But I have found my own escape
  The time and tide defying,
And I can travel in my mind
  I join the wild geese flying.

Iris Hesselden.

WEDNESDAY — NOVEMBER 16.

FOLLOWING a massacre in South Africa the writer Laurens van der Post summed up the response of the survivors:

"We prayed so that all bitterness could be taken from us and we could start the life for our people again without hatred. We know out of our own suffering that life cannot begin for the better except by us all forgiving one another.

"For if one does not forgive, one does not understand; and if one does not understand, one is afraid; and if one is afraid, one hates; and if one hates, one cannot love. And no new beginning on earth is possible without love . . ."

MAKING A
SPLASH

THE FRIENDSHIP BOOK

<u>THURSDAY — NOVEMBER 17.</u>

HELEN was getting over a bad bout of flu. When the Lady of the House went to visit her, she was surprised to see a rather battered rag doll sitting among her numerous get-well cards.

She noticed the puzzled expression and laughed. "It's on loan from Emily, the little girl next door," she explained. "You see, her mother had told her that I hadn't been well, and as Rosebud is Emily's favourite doll, she insisted on bringing her round to cheer me up until I felt better. And it's certainly succeeded, I must say — Rosebud makes me want to smile every time I look at her cheery grin!"

It made the Lady of the House smile, too. Now, doesn't this just go to show that a little act of thoughtfulness can be almost as effective as any medicine from a bottle?

<u>FRIDAY — NOVEMBER 18.</u>

I LIKE what Abraham Lincoln is reported to have said when he was asked about one of his associates.

"I don't like that man," he observed, "so I must get to know him better."

Sometimes we tend to acquire a hasty viewpoint of somebody and hold on to a certain feeling of dislike. Then, later, we are quite likely to change our mind when we get to know him or her properly.

We should always spend time getting to know others better. After all, first impressions can be so wrong!

SATURDAY — NOVEMBER 19.

ROADWORKS can be annoying with many delays for motorists, but sometimes they can lead to an unexpected and delightful detour.

This happened to friends in the north-east of England. They were travelling towards Barnard Castle, but were diverted due to repairs.

They drove along a road they hadn't used before and were pleased to happen upon a breathtaking view of Egglestone Abbey. The ancient ruins were nestling in a green and peaceful valley, a world away from the busy main roads.

As in life, our plans don't always go smoothly, and we must be prepared to change our route. Never be afraid of the detour. Who knows what you may discover?

SUNDAY — NOVEMBER 20.

THE Lord is my shepherd; I shall not want.

Psalms 23:1

MONDAY — NOVEMBER 21.

IDEAL COMPANION

LET optimism guide you
On the wary road through life.
If it's there beside you,
It may lessen care and strife.
Its timely intervention
Can often work to show
A practical dimension,
Wherever you may go.

John M. Robertson.

TUESDAY — NOVEMBER 22.

*M*AKE *me a good gardener, O Lord,*
In the garden of my life.
Let me sow the seeds of life.
Let my words be good and fruitful.
Let my ideas be sound and fertile.

George Appleton.

If we see our life as a garden then it becomes our duty to till and care for it. Now, let's get busy with the hoe, before the weeds take over!

WEDNESDAY — NOVEMBER 23.

THE clergyman in a certain parish used to stay now and then with a country shepherd whose work often took him out for long days and nights on to the hills.

Every morning the countryman would slip out of the house, and when his visitor asked why, he replied, "I go out to stand on the hillside and take off my cap to thank God for the beauty of this world."

I myself have not forgotten a visit to a village on the edge of the New Forest. How beautiful it all was — the landscape and the vista. The poet W. H. Davies was right when he wrote:

"What is this life, if, full of care, we have no time to stand and stare?"

A 19th-century diarist by the name of Henry Frederic Amiel mused: "I find a charm in rainy prospects: the dull colours are more velvety, the flat tones grow more tender. The landscape is like a face that has been weeping; it is less beautiful, certainly, but more expressive."

THE FRIENDSHIP BOOK

I READ a biography of L. S. Lowry and learned that the world might not have had the pleasure of seeing his many paintings and sketches if he hadn't missed a train to Manchester.

When coming down the steps from the platform, he saw in front of him the Acme Spinning Company's mill and knew immediately that he had to paint the industrial scenes of the North because no one else had.

During the first couple of decades that he painted, Lowry tried to hide the fact that he was upset because neither his mother nor the public seemed to like his work: fame didn't come to him until his later years.

What a good thing for us all that he missed that train!

HAVE you ever heard of Anne Bradstreet? Born in Northampton early in the seventeenth century, she was one of the earliest colonists to sail to the New World. Together with her husband, she faced many troubles, yet never lost her faith. She also managed to bequeath a legacy of poetry.

"If we had no Winter, the Spring would not be so pleasant," she wrote. "If we did not sometimes taste adversity, prosperity would not be so welcome."

Wise words which, even four hundred years after they were written, still hold a message for us today.

SATURDAY — NOVEMBER 26.

THERE'S a house in Birmingham, Alabama, which draws many visitors, each inspired by a poem that was written there. Its author Samuel Ullman, a businessman, became a writer in his seventies and wrote a poetic essay called "Youth".

Years later, his poem became a favourite of General Douglas MacArthur when he was Supreme Allied Commander in Japan. He pinned the poem on the wall of his office in Tokyo and he often quoted it in his speeches. The words are credited with inspiring a generation of Japanese citizens as they rebuilt their country.

Samuel Ullman's writings included this: "Youth is not a time of life; it is a state of mind; it is not a matter of rosy cheeks, red lips and supple knees; it is a matter of the will, a quality of the imagination, a vigour of the emotions; it is the freshness of the deep springs of life."

SUNDAY — NOVEMBER 27.

BE strong and of a good courage; be not afraid, neither be thou dismayed: for the Lord thy God is with thee whithersoever thou goest.

Joshua 1:9

MONDAY — NOVEMBER 28.

SOME of the prayers of famous Christians are still as appropriate today as when they were first written. One such was penned by John Bunyan, the author of "Pilgrim's Progress":

"There is nothing like faith to help at a pinch, faith dissolves doubt as the air drives away mist — let it rain, let it blow, let it thunder, let it lighten, the Christian must still believe."

THE FRIENDSHIP BOOK

GUESTS

I SET the table full of food
   And here they come, my hungry brood,
All flocking down with eager haste,
   And not a morsel goes to waste.
A blue tit, swift on dancing wing
   Is first to find the peanut string,
And then a robin, bold and bright
   Is quick to feed — and quick to fight!
More mannerly, a song thrush calls
   To glean the fruit and fat that falls
While finches swoop with joyful speed
   At any sight of sunflower seed.
A blackbird's choice is apples, sweet,
   Yet sparrows care not what they eat
But gorge as long as food is there
   Then fly away without a care.
No "thank you" ever comes my way
   For all the meals I set each day,
But my reward is in their song —
   I'm serenaded all year long!

                              Margaret Ingall.

I CAME across these words from Pam Brown and I would like to share them with you:

"Every kindness spreads in a shining circle — see how good people everywhere set rings of light moving across the darkness, rings that link and interlock and keep at bay the forces of the night."

When we are troubled and the world seems a sad place, I think they are worth remembering.

December

I WALK along quickly, a brisk, cheerful pace
And people smile back at my going-out-face.
They don't know the problems, the worry within,
The muddle my life is, just where to begin.
But seeing them smiling makes me cheerful, too,
Perhaps I've discovered the right thing to do.
And so I reach home and I start to unwind,
And search once again for new peace of mind,
Tomorrow, once more, I shall join in the race,
I'll put on my coat and my going-out-face!

Iris Hesselden.

CONSIDER these points to ponder which I found in an article called "All I Need To Know About Life I Learned From Trees":

It's important to have roots.
In today's complex world, it pays to branch out.
If you really believe in something, don't be
afraid to go out on a limb.
Be flexible so you don't break when a harsh
wind blows.
Sometimes you have to shed your old bark in
order to grow.

How true, don't you agree?

SEASON'S
SPLENDOUR

SATURDAY — DECEMBER 3.

ONE of the secrets of happiness is contentment, accepting and enjoying each stage of life as it comes. We don't want to be like the man who said, "I wish now I was what I was when I wished I was what I am now!'

Yes, some folk are never satisfied, are they?

SUNDAY — DECEMBER 4.

THY word is a lamp unto my feet, and a light unto my path.   Psalms 119:105

MONDAY — DECEMBER 5.

ONCE more I have been reading Great-Aunt Louisa's scrapbooks and diaries. An early December entry reads:

"Very cold today, I picked a few roses in bud in the garden this morning and put them in water on my writing desk. They will slowly open in the warmth of the room, and give much pleasure, with their scent and colour reminding me of Summer.

"Another kind of 'roses in Winter' is even more precious. When life seems dull and unprofitable and all is grey and lacklustre for you, those small concerned attentions you receive from others are indeed 'roses in Winter'. They comfort and encourage you to remember that it is a strange grey sky, which sooner or later doesn't turn to blue."

The diary entry ends with a miniature watercolour of roses in a vase. Apt thoughts for today, surely.

TUESDAY — DECEMBER 6.

WE all have to make big decisions in life and it is often tempting, when faced with a choice, to avoid risk by playing safe. David Lloyd George, the Welsh-born Prime Minister, drew on his own experience in Parliament when he gave this advice:

"Don't be afraid to take a big step. You can't cross a chasm in two small jumps."

Or as we might put it today, "Go for it!"

WEDNESDAY — DECEMBER 7.

I SAW a scene in the supermarket which made me smile. Two small boys were playing tag in the aisles as their mother coped with a toddler intent on taking things off the shelves.

When her attention was elsewhere for an instant there came an almighty crash. She turned to see her two red-faced young sons standing in front of a pile of fallen soap powder boxes. And what was the first thing the boys did? They pointed at each other and uttered those age-old words, "He did it!"

The young mother hadn't seen it happen, but wisely decided both boys were probably equally to blame. So she promptly marched them off to apologise to the manager and then told them to help put back the pile of boxes.

Surely Alexander Pope was right when he said: "A man should not be ashamed to own he has been in the wrong, which is but saying in other words, that he is wiser today than he was yesterday."

O COME ALL
YE FAITHFUL

THURSDAY — DECEMBER 8.

FEW people may recognise the name George Bramwell Evens, but some readers will certainly remember him as "Romany" of BBC Children's Hour during the 1930s and early 1940s. His interesting series of radio nature walks and his books made him a well-loved personality.

He introduced countless youngsters to the many lifelong pleasures of the countryside and the wonders of wildlife, though how he found time for it is something of a mystery for he was also a hard-working Methodist minister — first of all in Goole and Carlisle and then later he transferred to Halifax.

George Bramwell Evens was a simple man, one who was proud of his gypsy forebears and owned a traditional vardo — or caravan — which is still preserved more than 60 years after his death.

FRIDAY — DECEMBER 9.

SONG-TIME

LIFE'S too short to sit around
And moan about what's wrong.
From these actions comes the sound
Of such a plaintive song.

So let us change the tune and try
To banish fear and doubt,
And orchestrate as time goes by
There's much to sing about.

John M. Robertson.

SATURDAY — DECEMBER 10.

THE managing director of a large company has banned the words "I think" from his everyday vocabulary.

"The person who keeps saying 'I think' or 'I don't think' is simply beating about the bush," he told me. "There should be no doubt about whether or not you want something to happen."

On his desk I saw a card with these four lines of verse:

If you think you are beaten, you are,
If you think you dare not, you don't.
If you'd like to win, but you think you can't,
It's almost a cert you won't!

I think — sorry, I know! — you'll agree that this positive way of tackling any task is the sensible way to go about it.

SUNDAY — DECEMBER 11.

THE Lord is my strength and song, and he is become my salvation.

Exodus 15:2

MONDAY — DECEMBER 12.

THE Lady of the House made me smile when she told me of this letter, sent in good time for Christmas, by little Bethany, aged six:

Dear Santa: Could you come early this year? I've been really super good, but I don't know if I can last much longer. Please hurry.

Aren't we all a little impatient at times, and especially as we await the good things that the festive season brings?

TUESDAY — DECEMBER 13.

DO you know the golden eagle story? A man, who was a chicken farmer, found an egg which had rolled out of an eagle's nest. He took it home, popped it under a sitting hen, and eventually the eggs hatched out.

The young eagle found itself scratching around with a family of chickens. One day he looked up and saw a great eagle soaring in the sky above.

"That's a golden eagle, Monarch of the birds," he told the chickens, then went on scratching the ground like them, for that's what he thought he was. Little did he realise that he could have soared straight up into the sky.

Now, isn't that true of many of us? We remain earthbound instead of using our full powers and flying high. The Lord gave us talents and we should use them, whenever we can.

WEDNESDAY — DECEMBER 14.

THIS is the season when our thoughts turn to choosing words that will give a happy sparkle to festive cards. Consider this verse, chosen by the Lady Of The House to send to close friends:

We wish for you . . .

Comfort in difficult times,
Smiles when sadness intrudes,
Rainbows to follow your dreams,
Laughter to kiss your lips.

Sunsets to warm your heart,
Gentle hugs when spirits sag,
Friends to brighten your days,
Beauty for your eyes to see.

THE FRIENDSHIP BOOK

THURSDAY — DECEMBER 15.

THESE lines were written many years ago but are still true today:

If a child lives with encouragement,
*   He learns to be confident;*
If a child lives with tolerance,
*   He learns to be patient;*
If a child lives with fairness,
*   He learns what justice is;*
If a child lives with love,
*   He learns that the world is*
A wonderful place to be.

FRIDAY — DECEMBER 16.

ISAAC Newton is one of the great names in the history of science. He was an astronomer, a physicist and much else besides.

However, this modest man once said that, in his own eyes, he was like "a boy playing on the seashore, and diverting myself in now and then finding a smoother pebble or a prettier shell than ordinary."

In true greatness you will always find humility.

SATURDAY — DECEMBER 17.

I'M sure you know the story of Everybody, Somebody, Anybody and Nobody.

"Everybody was sure Somebody would do it. Anybody could have done it but Nobody did. It ended up that Everybody blamed Somebody when Nobody did what Anybody could have done."

Benjamin Franklin, the American statesman, said: "He that is good at making excuses is seldom good at anything else."

THE FRIENDSHIP BOOK

LET the heavens be glad, and let the earth rejoice: and let men say among the nations, The Lord reigneth.

Chronicles 1 16:31

THE rings of gold that we exchanged
Upon our wedding day,
Are symbols of the love we pledged
Forever — come what may.
All starry-eyed and so in love
We now were man and wife,
Ready for the challenges
Of blissful married life.

Times of laughter, smiles and fun
Rearing a family,
The teenage tantrums, tensions, tears
All weathered patiently.
And when the children had left home
We entered another phase,
Hobbies, interests, dreams and schemes
Took up all our days.

Looking back across the years
With soft and wistful smile,
I think back to our special day
When we walked down the aisle,
Oblivious to all around
We stood there brave and bold,
Acknowledging the love we shared
With simple bands of gold.

Kathleen Gillum.

THE FRIENDSHIP BOOK

TUESDAY — DECEMBER 20.

A T the time when Norway's constitution was being drawn up in the middle of the 19th century, it was decided that no more Jews would be allowed to enter the country. One writer was particularly appalled.

That Winter he composed a long poem about an old Jewish craftsman called Father Jacob who came over the border from Sweden every Christmas to sell his wooden toys. But this particular year each door is banged in the old man's face and he is hounded from village to village. A terrible snowstorm blows up on Christmas Eve and the following morning the people come out to find Father Jacob frozen to death in the drifts because there had been no place for him to shelter from the storm.

The Norwegian people recognised themselves in the poem and they felt ashamed. Their constitution was changed so that Jews were welcomed once more into the country. Truly the pen was shown to be mightier than the sword!

WEDNESDAY — DECEMBER 21.

I READ this text: "Two men looked through prison bars; one saw mud, the other saw stars."

In other words, one man was a pessimist who saw only the down side of life; the other was an optimist who saw only the bright side.

Even in a seemingly depressing situation, the optimist was able to see a glimmer of hope and encouragement and so, too, can we if we keep our eyes firmly focused on the One who is always there for us.

THE FRIENDSHIP BOOK

THURSDAY — DECEMBER 22.

I CAME upon this thought on a Christmas card, and would like to share it with you today:

May your neighbours respect you,
Trouble neglect you,
The angels protect you,
And Heaven accept you.

FRIDAY — DECEMBER 23.

FRANNIE Pew Hayes had a large family, including many grandchildren. Just before Christmas in 1984, to minimise the cost of presents, everyone drew another family member's name for gift giving.

Frannie's five-year-old grandson, David, drew her name, and asked what she would like. She chose paper clips and elastic bands! Protesting, he asked her to think of something else. With the Chinese Year Of The Bear in mind, she asked for a Teddy bear.

She was delighted by this first bear from her young grandson, and soon a collection began. Teddy bears multiplied, both from her own travels as well as gifts from family and friends.

Soon there were bears of all shapes and sizes and requests from people of all ages to come to see them started to pour in. The idea for a Teddy Bear Museum was born.

The Teddy Bear Museum in Naples, Florida is open to the public and, through donations and acquisitions, the number of exhibits has grown. The "Hug" of thousands of toy bears is viewed by many visitors worldwide.

SATURDAY — DECEMBER 24.

THE night before Christmas,
magic abounds,
Excitement is mounting,
wonderful sounds,
Bells in the belfry
are chiming good cheer,
The joy of having
the family near,
It's fun trudging over
crisp, crunchy snow,
The warmth of the fire,
Yule logs aglow,
Tomorrow's the day
our Saviour was born,
So long, long ago
on that special morn,
So simple the message,
soft on the ear,
Peace and goodwill
every day of the year.

Brian Hope Gent.

SUNDAY — DECEMBER 25.

WHEN they had heard the king, they departed; and, lo, the star, which they saw in the east, went before them, till it came and stood over where the young child was.

Matthew 2:9

MONDAY — DECEMBER 26.

LIFE is not measured by the number of breaths we take, but by the moments that take our breath away.

SKYLIGHT

TUESDAY — DECEMBER 27.

A GROUP of students, asked to list what they thought were the Seven Wonders of the World, chose, in this order: Egypt's Great Pyramids, the Taj Mahal, the Grand Canyon, the Panama Canal, the Empire State Building, St Peter's Basilica and the Great Wall of China.

Then the teacher noticed that one quiet pupil hadn't handed in her thoughts.

"I couldn't make up my mind because there are so many," she said. "But I think the Seven Wonders of the World are these — to touch, to taste, to see, to hear, to feel, to laugh and to love."

What a timely reminder of the things we tend to take for granted. Seven fine and deserving wonders, don't you agree?

WEDNESDAY — DECEMBER 28.

HERE is a small bouquet of words and thoughts, which I hope will brighten your day:

"Who loves a garden still his Eden keeps." These words were seen carved in the stonework of an old country garden.

"Earth laughs in flowers."

Ralph Waldo Emerson.

And when Winter seems to linger long, those lines written by Robert Browning remind us of Spring with its renewal and enchanting fresh life:

The year's at the Spring,
And day's at the morn . . .
God's in His heaven —
All's right with the world.

THURSDAY — DECEMBER 29.

A WORTHWHILE thought to consider today: "If you want to test your memory, try to recall what you were worrying about one year ago today."

FRIDAY — DECEMBER 30.

A TOP-FLIGHT businessman once surprised a seminar of executives by telling them, "No matter how bad trading is, if you lay aside the balance sheet and count your blessings instead, you will always be in profit."

He deserves his success.

SATURDAY — DECEMBER 31.

PERHAPS you would like to reflect on these lines — they seem particularly apt as the Old Year draws to a close. They come from two men, both writers and poets, whose lives were very different and spent some centuries apart, yet their words complement each other.

Abraham Cowley, once secretary to Queen Henrietta Maria, consort of Charles I, and a man who knew the turmoil of the English Civil War, wrote: "Enjoy the present hour, be thankful for the past . . ."

Then Scottish poet William Soutar, who spent so much of his adult life as an invalid, bade us all to "open your heart for the new life" of the New Year.

As this year ends the Lady of the House and I send our best wishes for all that is good during the next twelve months.

The Photographs

YESTERDAY, TODAY AND TOMORROW — *Norwich Cathedral.*
FROSTED FILIGREE — *Tummel Bridge, Perthshire.*
DEAR GREEN PLACE — *Glasgow University from Kelvingrove Park.*
STILL WATERS — *Nant Gwynant Pass, Snowdonia.*
FIRM FOUNDATIONS — *Whitby Abbey, North Yorkshire.*
MEADOW SWEET — *Gartocharn, West Dunbartonshire.*
SANCTUARY — *The University Church of St Mary the Virgin, Oxford.*
APPLE BLOSSOM TIME — *Gourock Park, Inverclyde.*
MIRROR IMAGE — *Looking towards Beinn Alligin on the track between Torridon and Inveralligin.*
BRIGHT OUTLOOK — *Tilberthwaite Beck, Lake District.*
HEAVENLY HARBOUR — *Crail, Fife.*
MONUMENTAL DISPLAY — *Scott Monument and Princes Street Gardens, Edinburgh.*
IDEAL HOME — *Fortingall, Glen Lyon.*
BUILT TO LAST — *Mannington Hall, Norfolk.*
ROCKS OF AGES — *Bempton Cliffs from Thornwick Bay near Flamborough.*
DISTANT HORIZONS — *Near Chilton, Oxfordshire.*
AS GOOD AS IT GETS — *Niarbyl, Isle of Man.*
BEST FOOT FORWARD — *River Wharfe, Yorkshire.*
STILL MILL — *St Monans, Fife.*
WHEN TIME STANDS STILL — *Childrey Village, near Wantage.*
WALK THIS WAY — *Rozelle Park, Ayr.*
HIGH AND MIGHTY — *Trossachs Forest Park.*
MAKING A SPLASH — *Hardraw Force, Yorkshire Dales.*
SKYLIGHT — *Great Edstone, York.*

ACKNOWLEDGEMENTS: **Marcello Aita;** Sanctuary. **Ivan J. Belcher;** Distant Horizons, When Time Stands Still. **Caledonia Light Images;** High And Mighty. **James D. Cameron;** Frosted Filigree. **E. W. Charleton;** Still Waters. **V. K. Guy;** Perfect Pal, Built To Last, As Good As It Gets. **T. G. Hopewell;** Apple Blossom Time, Walk This Way. **C. R. Kilvington;** Rocks Of Ages, Best Foot Forward. **Duncan I. McEwan;** Dear Green Place, Meadow Sweet. **Oakleaf;** Making A Splash. **Clifford Robinson;** Yesterday, Today And Tomorrow, Quiet Corner. **Robert Scott Photography;** Monumental Display. **Willie Shand;** Mirror Image, Ideal Home. **Sheila Taylor;** Nature's Harmony, Heavenly Harbour, Still Mill, Season's Splendour, O Come All Ye Faithful. **Richard Watson;** Firm Foundations, Safe Haven, Bright Outlook, Skylight.

Printed and Published by D. C. Thomson & Co., Ltd.,
185 Fleet Street, London EC4A 2HS.
© D. C. Thomson & Co., Ltd., 2004   **ISBN** 0-85116-856-6